Humble The Poet

UNLEARN
BENEATH THE SURFACE

101 Honest Truths
To Take Life Deeper

UNLEARN: BENEATH THE SURFACE WAS MADE POSSIBLE WITH
GENEROUS SUPPORT AND CONTRIBUTIONS OF THE FOLLOWING:

HARWINDER MANDER
SHALEEFA JUMA

TABLE OF CONTENTS

0. UNLEARN 2 HUMBLE STRIKES BACK?! 9
1. MY DADDY WAS A CABBIE 12
2. ARE YOU WORTH IT? 15
3. 2010 18
4. GET OVER YOURSELF 21
5. THE APOLOGY YOU NEVER GOT 23
6. IT WASN'T A GUN 26
7. YOU TERRIFY ME 29
8. TEACHERS 33
9. THE REAL FOUNTAIN OF YOUTH 35
10. NO MORE F*CKING VENTING 38
11. OPEN SAILS 41
12. SURVIVING ON THE INSIDE 44
13. LOVE OR FEAR? 47
14. HOW TO BE STUPID 49
15. MY APOLOGY TO DISNEY 52
16. LOSING OURSELVES 55
17. FANTASIES ALONE ARE FATAL 58
18. HAVE AN EASY LIFE, OR AN INTERESTING ONE 60
19. DRILL YOUR OWN HOLE 63
20. HAVING A STAKE IN THE OUTCOME 65
21. BEING EXTRAORDINARY 68
22. A WORLD OF IMAGE CRAFTING 70
23. BIG BELIEFS, SMALL THOUGHTS 72
24. HOPE IS A BEGGAR 75
25. POISON 77
26. DON'T TRY TO CHANGE PEOPLE 80
27. PAY THE COST 83

#	Title	Page
28.	DADDY'S IPAD	85
29.	THE OLDER I GET	87
30.	THE BEAUTY OF CONFUSION	89
31.	HERO TALK	91
32.	WE GET WHAT WE WANT	93
33.	TRINIDAD PART 1	95
34.	TRINIDAD PART 2	98
35.	MORE LESSONS WITH 50 CENT	102
36.	EXHAUSTED	104
37.	24 HOURS	106
38.	HACK AT THE UNESSENTIALS	109
39.	AYAHUASCA	111
40.	SHAME	122
41.	SUICIDE	125
42.	COURAGE	128
43.	HUMBLE THE HEDGEHOG	130
44.	UNSIGNED PERMISSION SLIPS	133
45.	LET'S TALK ABOUT SEX BABY	136
46.	LOOKS DON'T MATTER, PRESENTATION DOES	139
47.	I THREW A STONE AT GOD	141
48.	HEADS OUT OF THE CLOUDS	144
49.	COMMITMENT VS. INVOLVEMENT	147
50.	PRIORITIES	149
51.	YOU KNOW NOTHING HUMBLE PO	151
52.	F*CK YOUR RIGHTS	153
53.	POORA	155
54.	MILLION MILES A MINUTE	158
55.	F*CK YO CELLPHONE	160
56.	THIRST	162
57.	DOUBLE STANDARDS	164
58.	AWKWARD ART	166
59.	TOM HARDY	168

60.	WE DECIDE	171
61.	NO EXPLANATIONS NECESSARY	174
62.	CHRISTMAS: LILLY'S REVENGE	177
63.	SUGAR SHANE	180
64.	GOOD RIDDANCE	183
65.	WHAT CAN GO RIGHT?	186
66.	ALIGNMENT	188
67.	CO-EXIST	190
68.	NAKED	192
69.	PRISON BREAK	195
70.	THE INVISIBLE AUDIENCE	197
71.	MONKEY ON MY BACK	200
72.	LAW & ORDER	202
73.	MISTAKES	209
74.	QUESTIONS ARE BETTER THAN ANSWERS	211
75.	FIRST KISS	213
76.	IS IT WORTH IT?	215
77.	SAND IN YOUR HOURGLASS	217
78.	LEAN ON ME?	219
79.	THE CREATIVE BONE IS CONNECTED TO THE…	221
80.	SOMETIMES WE'RE THE BAD GUYS	223
81.	REBEL WITH A CAUSES	225
82.	PILLARS	228
83.	SIKH KNOWLEDGE	230
84.	HOLD LESS, BALANCE MORE	233
85.	A LESSON FROM L.A TRAFFIC	235
86.	ROLLERCOASTERS	237
87.	"AREN'T YOU HUMBLE THE POET?"	240
88.	THE TRUTH WILL NOT SET YOU FREE	243
89.	HUMBLE THE DANCER	245
90.	CHANGE YOUR SCRIPT	247
91.	WHERE YO REAL FRIENDS AT?	249

92. EXPLOITATION	251
93. TURNING THE PAGE	254
94. CURVEBALLS	256
95. RUN TO THE PAST	258
96. HUMBLE VS. LOVE	260
97. TWENTY-SEVEN AND NOT DEAD	262
98. MARKERS AND LABELS	265
99. GRAVITY	267
100. OSAMA	269
101. DUKH DARU	272

I don't know who you are, or how you came across me and my work, but I'd love to know

Please hit me up at
UnlearnBooks@gmail.com

Let me know a little bit about you, and what you think of the book

"THERE ARE NO SECRETS IN LIFE, JUST HIDDEN TRUTHS THAT LIE BENEATH THE SURFACE."

- MICHAEL C. HALL, *DEXTER*

UNLEARN 2
HUMBLE STRIKES BACK?!

In the first book I wasn't very personal, and that was for various (and what I thought were good) reasons. I didn't want to talk about myself for a whole volume – and who would like someone that did that? The original cover was an image that included my face, but I felt that the ideas were more valuable than the author. I wanted to share lessons and truths I learned. I have a way with words, and some ideas that I've been exposed to weren't seeing the light of day simply because they were packaged as too complex for others. My skill was being able to re-package ideas in a way that made them easier to digest and simpler to understand.

None of that meant the ideas were easier to apply to your life, and I'll stand by the age-old wisdom, "Anything worth doing won't be easy."

In this process of separating myself from the ideas, a bit of a creature was created of Humble the Poet. Many people saw me as the source of the wisdom, instead of simply the guy who can make it easy to understand. My inbox became flooded with people asking for help. People would have their mind made up about me before they met me.

"Oh you are much sillier than I thought, I always thought you were much more serious."

Well that's what happens when you write about heavy ideas, and have resting b*tch face. People will make reasonable conclusions.

I'm a very normal and painfully average human being. I was an elementary school teacher, and that taught me to simplify how I communicated so more people could understand me. Beyond that, the only way I could ever have anything to write about would come from my own life experiences and the feelings and emotions that come with it.

The truth is, I didn't write about myself at first because I both thought it was pretentious to assume anyone cared. And now that we've become a bit more acquainted with each other, I feel like it's time to show you another layer of myself.

And there won't be any more sequels titled, "The Third Layer," and "The Fourth Layer: Return of the Beardo" and corny spinoff books. The goal of this book is to remind you to go back to what you already know and scratch beneath its surface to see what's hiding underneath.

I just want you to become a digger, and if you can get through one layer, then I don't need to write another book to inspire you to keep digging.

But in order to inspire you to dig, I had to dig. And dig I did (read that 5 times quickly).

Beneath The Surface should feel both familiar and new. As with the first book, I do repeat myself sometimes, because nothing will stick if you only hear it once. Repetition is the key. This time though, I share a lot of what brought these ideas. I hope this helps you see who I am beneath the surface, as well as how simple it is to make these observations yourself, in your own day-to-day life.

In a nutshell, reading this book is like seeing me naked (and you didn't even have to buy me dinner), so let's not make this more awkward than it already is.

"...READING THIS BOOK IS LIKE SEEING ME NAKED (AND YOU DIDN'T EVEN HAVE TO BUY ME DINNER), SO LET'S NOT MAKE THIS MORE AWKWARD THAN IT ALREADY IS."

1
MY DADDY WAS A CABBIE

I couldn't have been older than four, hearing about the attack, and sneaking into my dad's room after I heard. He was sleeping when I went to see him,, and I crept up beside his bed to take a closer look at his face. On his forehead was a large gash and bump, which at the time seemed the size of a tennis ball. He had been attacked and robbed while driving his cab.

When he wasn't working his shifts, we would sometimes use the taxi as a family car. I remembered how industrial the back seat always felt, but it was always a cool experience because I would see the dials and buttons of his intercom radio. Now the cab felt even colder as a large glass shield was installed to protect the driver from the passengers. Now, it felt more like a police car than anything else.

That wasn't the last time my dad would be a victim of crime though. He experienced everything from punk kids running from paying their fare to crazy hooligans threatening him when he was simply parked on the street waiting for his next customer. For a long time there was a lot of anxiety every time he left the house to go to work. We don't realize how much anxiety we feel when we're young, simply because we don't know what anxiety is yet. We have no language for that kind of angst when a loved one is in danger.

My father has a masters degree in economics that he got from Jaipur University in Rajasthan, India. He came to Canada in the early seventies and married a few years later. He worked in a furniture factory for a few years before settling as a taxi cab driver by the time I was born in the eighties. He never pursued a career based off his education, because his education wasn't recognized in Canada. I imagine the City of Toronto probably has the most educated cabbies in the entire world.

As the years went on, he was able to move over to driving the fancy cabs at the airport, then when he returned to city driving, he would only work while the sun was still up. I still remember winter nights when it got dark early, worrying about what might be happening. I worried a lot when he wasn't home at the times that I was used to.

As every kid does this, but I often fantasized about making a lot of money, and then smashing his cab so he never had to leave for work again. For the longest time, I thought I did this because I wanted to impress my dad, later on I realized it was more to protect myself.

My dad is retired now, and I still get nervous when he goes for walks. I imagine him walking down the wrong side of the street and running into the wrong group of people, and the wrong things happening. I worry that the more popular I become, the more security we need at the family house. I worry that the over thirty years he spent sitting in a cab will have had a negative affect on his health. There are a lot of things to worry about.

But now, those worries don't paralyze me, they motivate me. I want my father to know that all the sacrifices he made, and bullshit he went through wasn't for nothing. I'm motivated to create a better life for him more so than I am for myself. I want him to see that what he did put me in a position to not only pursue higher education, but to also abandon it, take risks, and elevate myself to heights so few get to realize.

We're all motivated by different things, and we all experienced different types of traumas that shaped us throughout our lives. My story is nothing unique, and I hope sharing it will help you, the reader, find your flame to move forward, and create a life of your highest potential.

"WE'RE ALL MOTIVATED BY DIFFERENT THINGS, AND WE ALL EXPERIENCED DIFFERENT TYPES OF TRAUMAS THAT SHAPED US THROUGHOUT OUR LIVES."

ARE YOU WORTH IT?

Everything written from this point on is worthless if you don't believe you're worthy of hearing it. The further you read, the more you may find yourself questioning if you're worth it.

The answer is yes.

This is where our emotions and thoughts meet together and have a consensus that we deserve to have and be better. It's surreal to imagine ourselves in better situations sometimes. It may only feel like the life we want can only exist in our dreams, because that's the only place they've lived up to this point. The amount of fear in the process of converting dreams to reality is immense, and the first step to dealing with this is believing that you deserve to take this journey.

We are not average, we are evolved, and have a universe of ridiculous potential within us. The odds of our birth have already shown that we are capable and deserving of more, the only person in our way of realizing this is ourselves.

This book isn't about empty words and mantras, and I won't ask you to stare in the mirror screaming affirmations (though that will probably help). This book, and the truths in it, is about way more than just believing. This book talks about knowing through understanding. This book is not about ignoring the negative voices that exist outside and within, this is about staring them in the eye and saying out loud, "I disagree, I am worthy of having some amazing in my life, I already have amazing in my life, and I'm going to spend the remainder of my days realizing, amplifying and multiplying those amazing things."

Believing you're worth it doesn't mean these amazing things are going to arrive, but it does mean you will give yourself the effort you deserve to make things happen. Positive thinking doesn't automatically light the fire, it just motivates you to pick up the twigs and stick with it until happens, no matter how long it takes.

Your struggles are real, and if you thought reading this book will make things easier, you got the wrong book. I'm not here to sell you the idea that anything can be easy, but I am here to remind you that you're worth the difficulties that come with improving your life.

"I'M NOT HERE TO SELL YOU THE IDEA THAT ANYTHING CAN BE EASY, BUT I AM HERE TO REMIND YOU THAT YOU'RE WORTH THE DIFFICULTIES THAT COME WITH IMPROVING YOUR LIFE."

3

2010

"Mr. Singh, my mom saw you on TV, and I saw you on YouTube, and you were swearing"

That was the extent of my celebrity back then, it had been a year since I started performing spoken word and music around Toronto, and on a local level, I gained some attention. I was teaching third grade at Highfield Jr. School, the second largest elementary school in Toronto, and a five minute drive from the house I grew up in. Most of the kids I worked with looked like me in some way. They were Canadian born children to over-educated immigrant parents who worked labour jobs in a country where their skills and accreditations would not be recognized without further schooling (which meant a lot more tuition fees, too).

Life was hectic, I worked full time as a teacher, I would tutor middle/high school kids in math after for extra cash, I was in relationship with a girl I felt madly in love with, and I was releasing music as Humble The Poet, and getting recognized for it. This meant very little sleep, but I was managing, or so I thought.

Then the summer hit, I spent a week in Northern California staying with an artist by the named Mandeep Sethi. Everyone I knew in the creative field always had another full time hustle, they were students, had day jobs, or something else that kept their art a side passion, but not Mandeep. Mandeep lived alone in a rented bedroom in Daly City, and paid his bills from the random gigs he would throw or get. It was the first time I was exposed to that kind of hustle.

As a teacher, I had a salary that covered me for the summer, it was almost as if I was being paid to pretend to be a creative, the next paycheck was never an issue, and any money I made as Humble was just a great bonus.

But I watched Mandeep wake up early, stay up late, and work his ass off in between and it both scared and inspired me. There was no way I wanted to do this, there was no way my art wouldn't be compromised if I did, I would only leave the safety of my day job if I was offered more money than I was making a year as teacher.

It was cute to play full time artist for a few months, but September came back around, and it was time to get back to the real world, except this time, the real world no longer felt real. My reputation amongst my colleagues at school was that I was a nice guy, but pretty lazy. That was a stark contrast to the hustle reputation I had amongst my peers in the art scene. How could I be lazy in one world, but not another?

By October, the flame was gone, I couldn't bear to be in the classroom anymore, my wonderful girlfriend moved overseas, and then broke up with me a week later, a bunch of financial decisions I made, left me five figures in debt, and a miscommunication led to me losing one of my closest friends and collaborators.

October was also the month that I released a song by the name of Baagi, my biggest release to date, the song was written over the summer in a dorm room in NYU, right by Union Station. I used to brag about the beat before I even had a hook, I knew it would be a game changer for me, and it totally was. Up until that moment I didn't have any faith that this could be more than simply a side thing, I was always looking for outside validation to convince me it could be more. Releasing Baagi did just that, and I jumped on every opportunity I could thinking I "had made it".

By November, I was making arrangements to take a leave of absence from my job. I stopped tutoring, gave up the car I was driving, and began working with a local producer who promised to get me some paid work through the label he was with. It didn't matter if the story was true or even believable, I wanted to believe it, I was heart-broken, in debt, uninspired at work, and finally met someone who believed in me enough to want to invest in me.

By December I was gone. No more Mr. Singh, and hello Humble The Poet. It was my death in more ways than one.

"IT DIDN'T MATTER IF THE STORY WAS TRUE OR EVEN BELIEVABLE, I WANTED TO BELIEVE IT…"

4 GET OVER YOURSELF

We think about the big picture or the grand scheme of things very often, but an individual existence can't even register as a speck on the timeline. On Our Own, we're simply a drop of a vast ocean that will dry up in the sun, so why do we take ourselves so seriously? There are more stars in the sky than grains of sand on the earth, and much more empty space in between. We can fly a plane around the planet in forty four hours, but it would take over a thousand years to fly around the largest known star in our galaxy. We are so insignificant, but for some reason we internalize everything as if we are the center of this vast universe.

The goal of this chapter isn't to make you feel minuscule, it's to remind you that you already are, and to get over yourself. Trust me, life will feel much better that way. I understand and respect that your worst day is your worst day, and even though it doesn't compare to the worst day of others in say, a war-torn part of the world, you have a right to feel impacted. Those feelings are normal, even dwelling over them for extended periods of time is normal as well, but that doesn't mean it will benefit you.

This universe is vast and amazing, and you're a part of it, which also makes you vast and amazing. Appreciate that. Remember that your existence in the form you have is very limited, and it's not worth wasting time and taking everything so seriously. Feel light, enjoy life, we won't be here forever.

Get over yourself to enjoy the life you have.

"THIS UNIVERSE IS VAST AND AMAZING, AND YOU'RE A PART OF IT, WHICH ALSO MAKES YOU VAST AND AMAZING."

5

THE APOLOGY YOU NEVER GOT

A while back, I was deceived by a friend whom I took into my home. Not only did the lies affect me financially, I was also left with severe trouble trusting new people after I realized what had happened. Betrayal is a hard thing to deal with, and I went back replaying the moments of the relationship trying to see the warning signs in hindsight, and I found myself taking a lot of the blame for not picking up on clues earlier.

I'm not going to receive an apology or a resolution at this point. For all I know, that individual may not even think they did something wrong (everyone always has the best intentions apparently). What I had to come to realize is that the pain and resentment I carried with me was only hurting me even more than they ever could. I didn't notice that I was defining myself by the betrayal, and finding a comfort zone in feeling like a victim.

For my survival, I had to let it go.

'Life becomes easier when you learn to accept the apology you never got.' - Robert Brault

Eventually, it doesn't matter who was right or who was wrong, who betrayed whom and how, and that people know the story so they can see me as the victim. What's important is that I'm able to move forward in my life with the lessons I learned from that situation.

I was taken advantage of because I was in love with the lies I was being told, and that situation taught me to be more critical of things that came my way. And you know, that lesson in itself is a gift.
The pain is a part of the process, but it doesn't have to consume us. In order for us to move on, we have to decide to move on. The apology isn't coming, so we

have to accept what we have in front of us. Only then can we shed the weight of resentment that's holding us back.

Yesterday, and tomorrow will never be as real and important as right now. In order not to waste another present moment dwelling on the past, or even worrying about the future, we have to accept that apology we never got. Not to say we forget and forgive what was done with us, but instead to say, we want to move forward without it.

"IN ORDER FOR US TO MOVE ON, WE HAVE TO DECIDE TO MOVE ON."

6 IT WASN'T A GUN

"Chill!" Was the only word that came out of my mouth. I wasn't scared, at least I don't think . I think I was more in shock that this horrible thing was actually happening. This guy actually thought I was going to believe he head a gun in my face, and I could see it was something more like a cell phone. It didn't matter though. His only real job was to keep my attention long enough for the other two to come up from the side and start pounding me on the head.

I guess in a morbid way I'm proud I could take a few sucker punches and not fall. But you know what not falling means? More punches. And then punches turn into kicks once you finally do hit the ground.

"Chill!, I'm not from here!" I finally upgraded my sentence, but in hindsight, what was it that I was expecting? For them to take pity on me for not being a local? It was 2:30am on a street that borders two boroughs and I was casually strolling down an alley like stuff like this doesn't happen.
Before this started, I was chatting loudly on the phone without a care in the world. I even saw them from a distance, I could see them setting up, and by the time the first one approached me and so creatively said, "Give me all your money" my only reaction was to think, "This can't be happening, that's not even a real gun."

But you know, now then I was on the floor, in what felt like a pool of blood. I started murmuring, "Yo, I'm not from here, give me my phone back." And then one of them replied "Shut the f*ck up," as they all walked (not ran) away.

Why was I asking for my phone? It wasn't even mine. It was leant to me by a friend who worked at one of the big phone companies. It was one of those tester phones that I could pretty much use around the continent without worrying about long distance or roaming charges. In fact, everything they got their hands on, were things I was borrowing from friends, which is probably the reason I made my next irresponsible decision.

I got up and ran.

I wasn't running from them, I was running to my friend's apartment, which was only about 30 meters away. I banged on the door frantically. He opened it, he was in total shock when he saw my face, and he asked me what happened. My only reply was, "I got jumped, they're just around the block, we have to get that stuff back! We need weapons," and then I grabbed a knife.

He looked at me questioningly, "Are you sure this is what you want to do?"

"We have to get that stuff back. They're just around the corner." I said frustratingly, not realizing at the time that I was asking more from a friend than anyone should.

This was early 2011, the bubble I had been living in previously had officially burst, and I was suffocating on all that fresh air.

"...THE BUBBLE I HAD BEEN LIVING IN PREVIOUSLY HAD OFFICIALLY BURST, AND I WAS SUFFOCATING ON ALL THAT FRESH AIR."

7 YOU TERRIFY ME

When you all first suggested that I release a book of my writings, I thought it was a great idea, and it's rare for me to admit ideas that aren't mine are still great. I realized that in addition to taking your suggestions to write a book, I would need your support in making it, and I don't mean your moral support, I mean your money.

It isn't cheap to sit around all day, and do nothing but write, and it's scary to put yourself out there and ask for support to do just that. The doubt machine in my mind went into hyperdrive…. And it went something like, "Why would they give you money? No one cares about your work THAT much!" I was planning on crowd funding the book, and to do so meant I would be asking for your help.

It probably took me three months of procrastination and dilly-dallying to actually set up the crowd-funding page. I didn't know how much I needed, there's no price tag to writing a book, sure I had bills to pay, and I didn't know how much it was going to cost to build the book, but none of that mattered. What mattered was I was embarking on a new project and needed support to get it off the ground. So, I made up a number - sort of.

After leaving my job as a teacher, and racking up ignorant amounts of debt in hopes of catching my big break, the only way I was going to be able to deal with my lack of money was to sell everything I owned, including the condo I was living in. Selling it meant moving back home with my parents, which culturally isn't that big of a deal (I wasn't supposed to have left in the first place) but it was a defeat for me nonetheless.

I took the value of the condo at the time, and just divided by ten. I told myself if people would help me with 10% of what I lost, I would get that other 90% back. Getting that 10% would barely dent the financial problems I had at the time, but the amount wasn't meant to be practical, it was meant to turn a loss back into a win.

So now I had a goal of $23,758.00, and six weeks to do it, but I couldn't get myself to push the button to go live.

What if no one contributed? What if the project was a complete failure? I would crash and burn in front of everyone. I had witnessed other artists attempt to crowd fund, only to be told that they were selfish, and that their artistic projects weren't as important as charitable issues, and that children were dying around the world, and all of this while I wanted $23K to write a book?

But anyway, the button was pushed, and we went live.

Family and friends poured in contributions in the first week, it was heartwarming. One of my friends gave $100.00 and said his daughter would wear cloth diapers for the month, but it's worth it (I still hope he was joking).

I also made a list of people I knew I would have to reach out to individually. Making the list was interesting, you don't realize how many people you know until you take the time to write it down. But contacting people on the list- well, that's a whole other ball game.

More doubts came. They sounded like, "What if these people resented me for reaching out, and think I'm only their friends for a favour?" And, "What if I make them feel uncomfortable and awkward?"

I began sending texts, emails, and messages to people through social media. A lot of people ignored me, but then something very interesting happened. I began receiving some heavy contributions from people I didn't reach out to, people whom I only met once, at an event, or had a conversation with online.

This taught me two valuable lessons:
1. We don't know who's paying attention
2. As scary as asking for help is, it's always worth it.

Some of my millionaire friends never returned a call, while some of my fellow starving artists still mustered a few dollars just to feed the movement. It was an enriching experience, my victory wasn't the fact that we surpassed the goal and raised over $26,000.00, it was the fact that you all gave me the courage to ignore my doubts and push that button to go live.

I can't begin to express how important you, the readers, are to my life. The largest contributors (beside my mom) were mostly people I did not know, or hadn't known for more than six months. The wealth I received at the end of campaign was not the dollars and cents, but rather the realization that you have my back, and that is truly priceless.

Thank you.

That experience made me more confident, not only to put my work out there, but to put myself out there with it. This second book is a product of that. At one point, the thought of you terrified me, now all I want to do is share with you what's beneath my surface.

"THIS TAUGHT ME TWO VALUABLE LESSONS:

1. WE DON'T KNOW WHO'S PAYING ATTENTION

2. AS SCARY AS ASKING FOR HELP IS, IT'S ALWAYS WORTH IT."

8 TEACHERS

We have all been hurt by someone we cared about, whether that be a significant other, family member, business partner, or even a close friend. The pain of what they did to us is one thing, the feeling of being betrayed is just a whole extra world of hurt.

What hurts the most is the fact that we didn't expect these trusted people to have the capacity to hurt us. Those expectations are normal, and we want to let our guard down around the people we trust and care about, but sometimes people will exploit those situations.

There isn't a surefire way to avoid this, this is important to understand. Instead of developing trust issues and wasting life by remaining closed to new people, we can adopt a mindset of learning from our past and applying those lessons to our future.

The people who hurt us also teach us, and it pays to revisit and identify those lessons. There's wisdom to be gained from events where we may have made mistakes or allowed other people to take advantage of our closeness or friendship.

Respect yourself enough not to take these people back into your life. Sure, people can turn a new leaf, and they can definitely deserve second chances. That's on them though, and those new chances can be with new people, not you. We should be busy focusing our energy on those who deserve it. Let those who hurt you make the effort to re-earn it.

For us to grow, they may have to go.

"FOR US TO GROW, THEY MAY HAVE TO GO."

9 THE REAL FOUNTAIN OF YOUTH

I loved being in school, whether it was elementary or university. Every year was different from the last. New teachers, new friends, new classrooms, new environments, and new adventures. September was exciting and refreshing. It always felt like a new beginning, and all the experience felt new.

Once I left school as a student, and re-entered the classroom as a teacher, the experience was far different. Even though my assignments may change every year, it wasn't having the same impact. I really wasn't making new friends, and I was going to the same building day in and day out; things were becoming very repetitive. Even the holiday seasons became a blur. At one point, I made peace with this, and began the countdown of thirty-one years to retirement.

I wasn't getting enough new and stimulating experiences, and I chalked it up to being an adult. But you know what? I was wrong.

Once I left the safety and security of my day job, I felt like a child all over again. As Humble The Poet grew in fame (or infamy, I'm still deciding which one), I began travelling to new places, and making new life long friends. My experiences were brand new, and no two days were ever the same. The first book was written in 4 different countries, some days in a roach motel, other days on a friend's couch, and some on a plush bed in a fancy hotel.

I began to feel younger as time went on, even though I was getting older and (hopefully) wiser. What I realized was that I longed for the stimulation and adventure that I lost once I plugged myself in a routine of the workforce. These constant new experiences and stimuli made me feel like a child again.

And that's all it takes, new experiences and new stimuli. Time will blur once the days become repetitive, and we'll wonder where all the years went, because if every day is the same, very few of them will be worth remembering. Now, the past five years have felt more fulfilling and adventurous than the previous twenty-something combined.

Not all of us have the means or resources to hop on such an adventure in life. But to simply recognize that new experiences will either grant or continue our wondrous childhoods is something worth remembering. Children have an awe and enthusiasm towards life because everything is new, and many of the experiences are for the first time. No matter how old we are, we can still do things have these new experiences.

"When was the last time you did something for the first time?"

— John C. Maxwell

This very moment is the perfect moment to begin creating new experiences and feel the wonder and excitement of a kid again. Take a class, make a new friend, travel to a new location, do anything you're not used to, and feel your juices start flowing again.

I can promise you'll never want things to go back to "normal" again.

"THIS VERY MOMENT IS THE PERFECT MOMENT TO BEGIN CREATING NEW EXPERIENCES AND FEEL THE WONDER AND EXCITEMENT OF A KID AGAIN."

10
NO MORE F*CKING VENTING

Some of my days are so eventful, it feels like I've lived a week in an hour. Something wonderful can happen as soon as I get up, maybe a video is doing very well, or a new opportunity hits my inbox, or a cheque arrives in the mail. Those great moments give me the feeling that not only my day, but life in general is going to continue being great.

But then, like all highs, it slowly wears off over time, and I'm back to "normal."

At the same time, something not so pleasant can occur. It could be anything from waking up with a stiff neck, to having an argument with a loved one, or any other dip in fortune. Experiencing those can easily affect my outlook on the day, and life, as very pessimistic.

And unlike the highs, these lows don't wear off as easy, even when something wonderful happens again, it doesn't feel like I can quite right get back to normal.

The highs fade and the lows last. It's like when 99% of the people around you are wonderful and supportive, and 1% say something negative, the negativity seems to stick, and it's much trickier to shake off, even if more positivity follows.

This seems to be the nature of things, and almost all of us experience it, it seems easier to fall off the peak, than to climb out of the valley.

So what can we do? Well for starters, we can make an effort not to feed the negativity, and that means no venting.
Though we feel like venting helps us blow off steam, what it can really end up doing is digging our hole even deeper. While we're complaining or venting, our

minds are remained on the negatives, which is only going to make it harder to get ourselves out again.

No matter what happened in our day, no matter how horrible it was, there were tiny victories, and moments of positivity. We need to seek those out, and if we're going to spend energy and time reliving and sharing what we're experiencing, focusing on those positive moments is basically our only hope of mental survival.

Sure I missed a flight, had to deal with a rude customs officer, and won't get to check into my hotel for another four hours, but you know what? I did discover a great little Thai restaurant down the street that makes the most delicious food. And what's more, the waitress was cute.

It's important to share ourselves with others, let's just not burden them with our negatives. It doesn't help anyone.

We can look at life as a series of fortunes and misfortunes, or we can view every moment as an opportunity to learn and grow from. If things aren't going our way, and we find ourselves in a hole, at the very least, let's not make things worse by digging ourselves even deeper.

As an experiment, take a month off from venting, no matter how bad your day went. Try sharing the positive elements of it, and see it affects your overall mood and outlook on life.

"NO MATTER WHAT HAPPENED IN OUR DAY, NO MATTER HOW HORRIBLE IT WAS, THERE WERE TINY VICTORIES, AND MOMENTS OF POSITIVITY."

11 OPEN SAILS

I just sat through an MBA class at Harvard. Why is Humble at Harvard, you ask? I'm not quite sure myself. I simply left my sails open and let the wind take me. After crowd-funding the first the book, one of my largest contributions came from Boston, from a Harvard business professor named Karim. As a perk for the contribution I offered to come to Boston and do a private performance for him, and any guests he wished to bring. He in turn extended an offer for me to stay with him and his family in Cambridge, and I accepted. I had an amazing experience, and met a great group of people who have shown me a lot about the business aspect of being who I am.

This isn't the first time I've accepted invitations from people I don't know, let alone haven't previously met. I once left a wedding in Oakland with a guy I met an event to go partying in San Francisco. It was a crazy night, and then he and his friends dropped me back off to my hotel, and I never heard from him again.

I once accepted a show request in Chandigarh, India based on an email, I travelled there alone and ended up making amazing friends, who have not only helped me, but have also helped my own friends have more opportunities in India.

I've accepted an invitation to attend a furniture show after receiving an email from a supporter who wanted me to see their designs. That experience made us friends, and I ended up performing in the gallery he built years later, and staying in his home in Calgary.

I've accepted numerous invitations around the world, and as a result, I've not only had random and enlightening adventures, I've often made life long friends, and had experiences I would never forget.

All of this happened simply because I kept my sails open, and let the wind of life take me where I needed to go.

I'm not big on fate or pre-destiny, but I do think we should be open to new experiences, because they will take us out of our comfort zones and help us evolve.

You don't have to accept invites from strangers in foreign cities to have the same experiences, simply be open to the idea of trying new things, it could be something that breaks you from the normal routine of your day, or something completely wild and adventurous. Trying something new is the best way to ensure that new things are encountered and we stay stimulated.

Where does the wind want to take you today?

"TRYING SOMETHING NEW IS THE BEST WAY TO ENSURE THAT NEW THINGS ARE ENCOUNTERED AND WE STAY STIMULATED."

12 SURVIVING ON THE INSIDE

We know what we need to survive in the outside world: Food, clothes, shelter, oxygen, water, wifi (okay, maybe not wifi, but it's almost essential). But are any of us exactly sure about what we need on the inside? What is required for us to survive within?

Some people would call this feeding the soul, I don't know if it's the soul or the ego that needs feeding, but there are definitely needs and urges that exist inside of us that guide us to make the decisions that we make.

I struggle with this, because I may identify a need within myself, but not notice anyone else chasing that same thing. Sometimes that's acceptance, or love, or validation or art. Do we all have different inner needs? Are they even needs to begin with, or are they simply wants?

Some think it's art, and it's a decent argument if you think about it.

I got into the creative world because I know it was ripping me apart inside to get my ideas and expressions out, and I learned that the stress of that alone can cause real life health problems.

That creativity can manifest itself as a new way to build a tool, or a building, or a gun, or a poem, or song, or an app to play while you sit on the toilet.

There's a lot of creativity on the planet, and maybe taking things in isn't necessarily what we need to feed our inner self, but instead the opposite, Maybe we need to put more things out there.

Creating, contributing, leaving something behind are things our twisted wires are guiding us to do. For some it may be having children, for others it's a fresh new invention, and for me, I feel quenched when a spark in my mind comes to life in front of me and makes itself into a poem, a line of words in a book, or a song I know I'm going to get to share when it's finished.

What do you need to create to survive?

"THERE'S A LOT OF CREATIVITY ON THE PLANET, AND MAYBE TAKING THINGS IN ISN'T NECESSARILY WHAT WE NEED TO FEED OUR INNER SELF, BUT INSTEAD THE OPPOSITE, MAYBE WE NEED TO PUT MORE THINGS OUT THERE."

13
LOVE OR FEAR?

The things that motivate us can also serve to confuse us. Sometimes we may not know why we're doing the things we're doing. Are we motivated by love, or is it fear? Both are strong emotions and ideas, and both have the uncanny ability to light a flame in us to make us move forward. The issue isn't which one is nobler, or even which one is better, but rather how to become aware of which of these two things is a driving force in our lives.

Are we chasing our passions and the things we love, or are we living a life that allows us to avoid our fears entirely. These concepts are not polar opposites. Fearing rejection, and loving attention can go hand in hand, and wanting one may also fuel wanting to avoid the other, and it's up to us know what's happening and when.

Depending on your beliefs, this may be the first of many, or it may be only life you get to live. Regardless of what you believe, having a life where fear is a continual theme could rob you of a wealth of experience that could feed the things we truly love about our life. We may be denying ourselves an amazing life simply because we're afraid to be uncomfortable and try new things.

Don't confuse this fear with the type of fear necessary for survival. Humans have this uncanny ability to create our own fears, especially when it comes to the unknown. Often our fears can be illogical, but the same could be said for love, and some of the most amazing people use that illogical love to accomplish amazing things.

Are you waking up in the morning with excitement or fear, if it's not the answer you wanted to hear, what can YOU do to change that?

"WE MAY BE DENYING OURSELVES AN AMAZING LIFE SIMPLY BECAUSE WE'RE AFRAID TO BE UNCOMFORTABLE AND TRY NEW THINGS"

14 HOW TO BE STUPID

I, like everyone else, get lost in my past, and start kicking myself over the stupid things I've done. Realizing that there's little benefit to regret, I decided I wanted to learn something, not just from my individual mistakes, but from all of them in general.

That's when I realized how to be stupid.

We all make mistakes and that's normal, human if anything. The mistakes we make in life are the opportunities we have to learn lessons and convert our experiences into to wisdom. But sometimes we're just plain stupid.

Stupidity isn't making a mistake, it's when we refuse to look at some of the obvious long term outcomes of our decisions because we're fixated on what we'll receive in the form of short term gratification.

Hot sauce comes to mind. For many, having added spices with their meal, though wonderful at the time, can lead to some uncomfortable consequences later. These consequences are things we may have experienced multiple times in the past, but for some reason disregard for that immediate experience of a tasty meal; this, ladies and gentlemen, is how to be stupid.

As young people, some of us may not have many years under our belt to see the long-term picture. We may not realize how the decisions we make now can have an affect on us in the next 30-40 years. That lack of foresight isn't necessarily stupidity, but refusing to develop that foresight is.

In my own life, I realize the stupidest things I did often related to finding the path of least resistance. I was constantly suckered in by promises of big things, and little effort, refusing to acknowledge that if it things sound too good to be true, they probably are. This type of stupidity on my part resulted in ridiculous purchases, investments, and life choices and of course, relationships. What made this stupidity for me, wasn't that the choices were simply ridiculous, but more so, that I made an effort to ignore the pattern in my own behavior, hoping the next choice was going to be the exception and not the rule.

Whether it's smoking cigarettes, or eating unhealthy, or living a lifestyle beyond our means. If we're purposefully ignoring the long-term consequences of our actions for some short-term smiles, we're on the stupid train. Things will always sort themselves out, but that doesn't mean they will for our benefit. The goal here isn't to make us feel stupid, it's to simply promote awareness of when we may be making unnecessarily stupid choices that can have long term damage to lives we have.

One of the best ways to wise up is to learn and recognize how to be stupid.

"ONE OF THE BEST WAYS TO WISE UP IS TO LEARN AND RECOGNIZE HOW TO BE STUPID."

15
MY APOLOGY TO DISNEY

I've done a fair amount of writing dedicated to the fact that some of our distorted views of reality, especially related to love and other emotions, have come from Disney movies. And you know what? I still they think they are. What many people in North America and abroad understand about romance can be equated to movies, and Disney has done a great job of perpetuating myths and stereotypes that do us no good.

But then they made *Inside Out,* which is a fascinating movie that explains emotions in such a way, that everyone from child to an adult can grasp and understand the content. I was in awe of this movie, and I'm happy that it exists. It does, however, totally kill my ability to make the argument that Disney movies are the enemy.

So Disney, I'm sorry, but kinda not really. One dope movie doesn't totally make up for your track record but I see you're heading in a better direction, and I'm excited to see what your work contains next.

The idea of love being an object we receive isn't exclusive to the movies, romance novels, and other escapist media. It also exists within the family structure where our parents tried there very best to love us unconditionally. But nobody shows us the toll that type of love really takes.

We became so entitled to love, that by the time our parents made it apparent that the love and support they provide us comes at a cost (and isn't as unconditional as we thought), it becomes so hard to grasp, and in a lot of cases we rebel, and seek that type of love we've grown accustomed to elsewhere. As I've mentioned before, love is a gift, not a loan, and we shouldn't be giving it out in hopes of having it returned every time. We should be giving it because we have it to give. This is a critical idea to understand and respect if we want to have relationships that are lasting, and not fickle ones that leave us bitter when we don't feel our expectations are being met.

We all have expectations, good and bad, big and small, and before we can effectively manage, we may need to figure out where those expectations came from in the first place. Whether it was a Disney movie, the family structure, or just society as a whole and false promises we thought were made to us. Having that awareness will then set us up to better determine the expectations we want, and who best to meet them (hint: we can probably be the source of love we need ourselves).

I hope Hollywood, and especially Disney, continue to create dope content like 'Inside Out' because there are valuable lessons to be taught, and entertainment is a great medium to do it.

In the meantime I'll find someone else to pick on as the cause of our unrealistic expectations

"WE ALL HAVE EXPECTATIONS, GOOD AND BAD, BIG AND SMALL, AND BEFORE WE CAN EFFECTIVELY MANAGE, WE MAY NEED TO FIGURE OUT WHERE THOSE EXPECTATIONS CAME FROM."

16 LOSING OURSELVES

It would be a clichéd thing for me to say don't lose yourself if you want to keep someone else. We don't really realize we're making such compromises until we're knee deep into our messes. We may not have the best view of ourselves to begin with, so what's the big deal if we're changing constantly in order to impress people around us. Maybe it's an improvement. Right?

I'm fighting the urge to simply type W-R-O-N-G in bold letters and end this chapter.

We're all on a journey, a journey which is both on the outside in the world, and inside with the universe that exists inside of us. Although they seem like two very different places, exploring one will most definitely help us understand the other.

By losing ourselves, that can cause us to be lost to the world outside as well. Attaching our identity to anything external, including the approval of others, is dangerous because if we lose them, what will we have left?

It's considered noble, and even romantic, to bend and compromise for the happiness of others, but it comes at a price. If it's done long enough, we may trade in whatever beautiful clarity we could have realized for a bit of temporary comfort. That comfort won't fulfill us for very long, and to fill the void we don't understand, we may resort to decisions, which may be even more destructive.

Knowing ourselves (which is a lifelong journey) puts us in a situation to navigate both the world inside us, and the world around us. The clarity and direction that comes with that is a gift when it comes to creating relationships, because we can form deeper bonds and connections with others who have priorities similar to ours.

Being anything less than ourselves to feed our need for acceptance won't keep us full, or even sane, for very long. But like any craving, it can be curbed slowly, and overtime.

Remember, we can only be ourselves when we know ourselves, so let the exploration continue.

"BEING ANYTHING LESS THAN OURSELVES TO FEED OUR NEED FOR ACCEPTANCE WON'T KEEP US FULL, OR EVEN SANE, FOR VERY LONG."

17 FANTASIES ALONE ARE FATAL

When we fantasize, we spend more time focusing on the destination than the journey, that it can blur our ability to create a bridge to actually get there. Dreaming and meditating on flat abs won't get us a better stomach. Thinking about the steps required to get to where we want to go (i.e. diet and exercise) and make a plan to implement those steps (i.e. creating a routine of diet and exercise) dramatically increases our chances to make it happen.

We're all excited when we think about our dreams coming to life, but how many of us maintain that enthusiasm when we think about everything it's going to take to get there? More important than knowing where we want to go is knowing where we have to start to make it happen. It's easy to want a million dollars, but it's not as easy to take a look at the money we have, and figure out how we're going to turn that into a fortune.

This is why the journey is more important than the fantasy, and why we have to continually reinforce our relationship with the reality of our current situation. When we know where we are, and know where we want to be, we can then plot the path to get there. That path is the more important thing to ensure our success.

"WHEN WE FANTASIZE, WE SPEND MORE TIME FOCUSING ON THE DESTINATION THAN THE JOURNEY, THAT IT CAN BLUR OUR ABILITY TO CREATE A BRIDGE TO ACTUALLY GET THERE."

18 HAVE AN EASY LIFE, OR AN INTERESTING ONE

As someone who's realizing their dreams every day, I can honestly say that everything is lollipops and gumdrops. Everyday isn't wonderful and full of bliss. I am not consumed with appreciation and happiness all the time, but that's ok, because happiness is not the goal, but the stimulation and inspiration totally is.

Chasing happiness in life seems to be a common goal for so many people. It's interesting because we wouldn't know what happiness was unless we were aware of all those other emotions, including the ones we consider negative and avoidable (i.e. sadness, anger, frustration, anxious, et cetera). All emotions are important to us, so we can't measure the quality of our lives with how happy we feel all the time; that really shouldn't be the goal.

Instead, we can focus on how stimulating life is. Every day can be an adventure, and not every part of that adventure is going to be pleasant, but it can be interesting. I can promise you if you work on creating the life you want, you definitely will not be happy every day. But you know what? You won't be bored, and maybe that's enough.

Staying engaged in anything keeps life fresh and our minds active. It also saves us from that feeling that time is flying by, because the days aren't so repetitive, that they simply blur together. When I was a teacher that was happening to me. Years would go by and I would have nothing new to show for it (besides a bigger tummy).

Now, I can assure you that my life is not happy all the time, but more importantly, it's never, ever boring. It's eventful, and everyday comes with new challenge, lesson, and experience.
So let's reframe our expectations, and realize that chasing smiles all the time makes little sense. If we were happy all the time, we'd probably forget what

happiness actually was. Happiness exists in contrast to the lows, and we need to feel the cold to know hot, the high to know the low, and the sad to feel happy. Focusing on a life of interest, and not judging the emotions we encounter, will be much more enriching and rewarding.

"EVERY DAY CAN BE AN ADVENTURE, AND NOT EVERY PART OF THAT ADVENTURE IS GOING TO BE PLEASANT, BUT IT CAN BE INTERESTING."

19
DRILL YOUR OWN HOLE

I'm in the Dominican Republic, and just finished attending a yacht party thrown by my uncle. Back in the 70's, he dropped out of high school, became a cab driver, then a truck driver, then he was a truck owner, then he owned a fleet of trucks, and right now he owns a fleet, a warehouse and a shipping yard. Getting a taste of the good life is nice. It's his son's wedding celebration, and he wants to share his happiness with his family. He rarely splurges, and on the rare occasion he does, it's to share with other people.

The rest of us are just visiting though. We're getting a taste of the life, but it's not a place we get to stay. Rather, we simply got a glimpse through the hole he's been slowly drilling for the past twenty to thirty years. When many were doing their nine-to-fives, he was taking risks, helping out others, and in the long run it paid off. For the rest of us trying to create the lives we want, we can either view him as a source of envy, or a source of inspiration.

Plenty of times in my career, I've been invited to the other side, where people have realized their dreams, but I was just a visitor. If I ever wanted to spend more time there, I would have to work on drilling my own hole.

When it comes to drilling your own hole and digging a path to the life you want, it can't be a race. Slow and steady ensures that you don't crack anything. It's nice to get a glimpse of what life can be like beyond our own dreams by poking our head through the progress of others, but it'll be much nicer, and more permanent, if we focus on our own path.

"WHEN IT COMES TO DRILLING YOUR OWN HOLE AND DIGGING A PATH TO THE LIFE YOU WANT, IT CAN'T BE A RACE"

20 HAVING A STAKE IN THE OUTCOME

War, crime, disease, environmental issues, corruption, inequity, inequality, discrimination, and the list continues... The world doesn't always look or feel like the most wonderful place to be. Focusing on these unpleasant elements can have a huge effect on our outlook towards our future and the future of our planet as a whole.

So what can we do to make sure we don't drown in a sea of despair? We can't fix any of these problems over night. If anything, many of these problems existed well before our time, and don't seem to be losing any steam. We can always be pessimistic about it, throw our hands up in defeat, declare that the world is going to hell in a hand basket, and live out our years jaded. Another option is that we try to become Captain Save-The-Planet, and devote our lives to eradicating all that we feel plagues our world. But with the magnitude of what's going on, both those options can leave us mentally, physically, spiritually, and psychologically exhausted.

So let's ask ourselves, are there any other options?

We don't have much control over the state of affairs, and that can be frustrating, but we do have some control in decide what elements of this existence. We can choose certain things to focus on in life and have a stake in the outcome.

Now, if the planet descends into WW3, we don't really get to decide whether we want to be affected or not, but for many of the other issues, we can decide to do something about it on our micro level, or acknowledge that most likely what happens is out of our control, and we have to focus our attention and stick our flag into whatever sand we feel is best.

Me? I'm frustrated that I have no control over the corruption of every government around the world. Some may make it their prerogative to combat this, but I haven't. That doesn't sound very heroic or romantic, but it is realistic. I have limited time on this planet, and I've decided to choose other priorities for my purpose on this planet, and for everything else I'm simply a member of the wider audience.

George Carlin said "When you're born you get a ticket to the freak show. When you're born in America, you get a front row seat," and it's totally true. Now, the rest is up to you to decide when we want to participate in the happenings of the world and when it's best to sit back in our seat and enjoy the show. That's not as pessimistic as much as it is honest. I can devote my life to saving the elephants, stopping global warming, equal rights for women and minorities, providing access to clean water to children around the world, or cleaning the local park in my neighborhood... But you know what? As much as I wish I could, I can't do them all.

We can do anything, but not everything, and that realization will save a lifetime of grief and frustration.

Like watching a basketball game, and not having a favourite team, having no stake in the outcome means all you want is an entertaining game. You get to choose how to sit in that seat.

"WE CAN DO ANYTHING, BUT NOT EVERYTHING, AND THAT REALIZATION WILL SAVE A LIFETIME OF GRIEF AND FRUSTRATION."

21 BEING EXTRAORDINARY

I love listening to the stories of people who have accomplished some amazing things. I'm not super interested in all the perks they receive from their success as much as I am about what they were willing to do to get to the positions they were in. I have yet to hear a story about being in the right place at the right time, or someone getting discovered. Instead I'm constantly hearing about people who went the extra mile, putting in efforts that were beyond what the average person would consider normal.

But that's the point, it's not about what the average person would do, it's about what an extraordinary person would do, and that will always be the farthest from normal. Extraordinary outcomes require extraordinary efforts, extraordinary risks, extraordinary determination, and an extraordinary mindset.

So do we check our pulse and see if we were born extraordinary? No.

We all have the option to be extraordinary, it's just a matter of deciding and committing to it. The outcomes won't happen overnight, or over a week, or even a month. The larger-than-life-stuff, requires a larger than life commitment, and you have to be in it for the long haul.

Depending on how old you are, that either sounds torturous, or like common sense. Regardless of your feelings about it, the facts won't change, and the shortest route to your extraordinary life is the one you begin.

So get started, reject being normal and average, and level up. I promise you it's worth it.

"EXTRAORDINARY OUTCOMES REQUIRE EXTRAORDINARY EFFORTS, EXTRAORDINARY RISKS, EXTRAORDINARY DETERMINATION, AND AN EXTRAORDINARY MINDSET."

22 A WORLD OF IMAGE CRAFTING

For the longest time, many of my decisions were focused on what looked good, what could be shared on social media to engage an audience, what could validate that I was actually doing something. This image crafting existed far before the internet. It's been important to us to project the illusion of success, or stability or happiness for some reason, even if that project didn't at all match reality.

In some sense, it can be the age old,"Fake it 'til you make it" idea. We need to give the impression that it's all good, even if it isn't. Worrying about appearing legitimate to others, instead of focusing on actually becoming legitimate, trapped me in a morbid loop where I wasn't making any real and tangible progress in my life.

We all put our best foot forward, it's normal, but if the priority is to jazz up our lives, "For display purposes only," then that's much-needed energy wasted that could be better spent. Real growth and progress takes time, and sometimes it can't be captured in a post for our invisible audiences, and most often that's not important at all.

Decorating our masks won't improve what we have underneath them. Instead, it'll just make us more dependent on those masks. When we have a clear focus on what we want from life, and work towards it without worrying about what other people think, eventually we won't need a mask, or have the urge to show off to others, fulfillment will be it's own reward.

Instead of crafting the image we want, let's craft the life we want, and understand all the images we see of others, are just as crafted, so comparing is pointless.We are better of prioritizing what we feel over what others see.

"DECORATING OUR MASKS WON'T IMPROVE WHAT WE HAVE UNDERNEATH THEM."

23 BIG BELIEFS, SMALL THOUGHTS

I think all my insecurities worked for the CIA at one point, because they always knew how to disguise themselves so well. After a few years of being Humble The Poet, I felt it was necessary to start putting other people on the platform I had made for myself in order to give them an opportunity.

I remember sitting with a producer named Dusty Loops and telling him about why I felt our friend B Magic would make such a star, "He's a great lyricist, he's got the look, and such an interesting back story, he can be a star, and take things to the next level."

"I think you just described yourself," replied Dusty, "Right now, you're in a better spot to become that star."

It struck me at that moment that the only reason I wouldn't make it any farther, is because I didn't believe I could. Hearing that outside validation from Dusty made a huge impact on my confidence and belief that I could take things to a new level.

That was 2010, and while my insecurities haven't melted away completely, they do wear some different masks. One of the challenges with writing this book was that I didn't have the confidence to finish a chapter and store it, knowing it was at the standard it needed to be. This was happening because I have been so used posting my work immediately after writing and receiving instant validation and feedback in the forms of likes, comments, and shares on social media. When writing for the sake of publishing, ink will stain the page with my words before I ever know if the public enjoys what they read.

A few years later, my friend DJ Nav UDN from the UK would put these feelings into words perfectly, saying,

"You are only as big as your beliefs, and as small as your thoughts."

If we don't believe we can do something, we probably won't be able to do it. I was waiting for outside validation before I had enough confidence take any risks to make things happen. What I wasn't realizing was that I was depending on that validation to decide how I would feel about myself, and that's a dangerous thing.

If we think small of ourselves, we'll remain small. The person that needs to believe in us the most is ourselves. The confidence that comes from believing in yourself isn't a delusional one. It's the foundation that allows you to deal with the challenges that will most likely come your way. Confidence isn't assuming everyone will like me, it's knowing I'll be ok if they don't. Confidence is knowing that I'm capable of anything if I work my ass off to achieve it.

Some of the greatest influencers of our generation had strongly held beliefs about themselves and their importance and purpose on this planet. They weren't hoping people would like them, instead they were hoping they could get out their contributions to the world because they knew it was important for both them and society as a whole. If they thought any less of themselves, very little would have been accomplished.

"I am the greatest. I said that even before I knew I was."
Muhammad Ali

Muhammad Ali doesn't have a perfect record (although he did avenge most of his loses), but he is still widely considered the greatest boxer in history. Before the outside world could see that, he had to see it in himself.

What are your thoughts? What are your beliefs? How big are they? How big are you?

"CONFIDENCE ISN'T ASSUMING EVERYONE WILL LIKE ME, IT'S KNOWING I'LL BE OK IF THEY DON'T."

24 HOPE IS A BEGGAR

When I think of hope, I think of a beautiful balloon floating around, just out of reach. It's wonderful to look at, but so delicate, that the slightest bit of reality will pop it. We all love hope, it's a motivator, and sometimes a main factor in helping us keep our composure, and that's definitely an important thing to think about.

We read about people in horrible situations that survived because, according to them, they never gave up hope. However, on a day-to-day basis for the rest of us, hope is that long four letter word we put in between where we are, and where we want to be.

We can very easily hope our lives away, and it can serve as something to prevent us from actually taking realistic steps to improve our situation. If we want things to happen, we can't simply hope and wish for them, we have to work for it.

In some senses, hope also indicates that we don't have enough confidence in who we are to handle things, and instead, we wish that things will work out on their own. Instead of having hope, I encourage you to have faith, not in the things around you, but in yourself. Don't believe things will work out, believe you can do what's necessary to make things work out.

"I don't believe in hope." he said. "Hope is a beggar. Hope walks through the fire and faith leaps over it." – Jim Carrey

"HOPE IS THAT LONG FOUR LETTER WORD WE PUT IN BETWEEN WHERE WE ARE, AND WHERE WE WANT TO BE."

25 POISON

The most damaging voice in your life is the one inside your head.

I don't know what horrible things other people spit your way, but that sh*t is only effective if it finds a voice within you to hold hands with. We let people treat us the way we think we deserve.

If you're talking down to yourself constantly, and then worrying, and then feeling guilty, you're filling your spirit with poison, and you're killing yourself slowly by doing so. Your thoughts literally become your life.

The voices inside your head have a strong impact on you, and sometimes you're going to need to say "SHUT THE F*CK UP" and change the dialogue. Tell yourself you're feeling awesome, and you'll feel a bit more awesome. This isn't the placebo, this is the real thing. Your emotions are based on your mindset, and often your mindsets are choices, choose happiness.

Decide what you want to focus on in your life, and decide the conversations inside your head. When good things are being said inside, the bullsh*t that may come from outside will have nothing to connect with.

"DECIDE WHAT YOU YOUR LIFE, AND CONVERSATIONS

WANT TO FOCUS ON IN DECIDE THE INSIDE YOUR HEAD."

26 DON'T TRY TO CHANGE PEOPLE

Unfortunately, none of my friends are perfect like me. All of them are wonderful people, but they could use a little advice to take themselves to the next level. Some could lose some weight, others could focus on their goals a bit more. Some of my friends would benefit from having me as their life coach. I mean, I love them just the way they are, but I'd probably love them more if, you know, they changed a bit.

The best way to avoid your own problems is to focus on the problems of others. Since nobody is perfect, there will be an endless amount of fix-me-up-friends to work on, while simultaneously ignoring our own personal follies.

People aren't projects, they're people - and like it or not, they come with flaws. We all have that friend who may be making life decisions that we don't agree with, some silly and immature, others can be destructive to both themselves and those around them. We care about them, and we want to help, but the people who will benefit from the most help are the ones that have already begun helping themselves.

I'm rarely the most successful person in the room, but I'm always down to help those who are doing better, simply because my energy never feels like it's gone to waste. Those who are less fortunate also need and deserve help, but the help we give them will be minimal if they're not putting in the majority of effort to help themselves.

That effort won't be inspired by nagging them, or giving them a lecture. People are rarely motivated through being told what they're doing wrong. If anything, that pep talk you had planned may push them away. People will change when they're ready, and only if they really want to. One thing I know for sure, it's not up to us to decide how others should live their journeys. That's a difficult reality to grasp especially if people we care about are causing themselves harm. I'm not advocating that we abandon them, but rather create an environment, and let them know that we're there to help them.

The energy we spend trying to change others is much better spent working to improve ourselves. That in itself will motivate others who may be uncomfortable taking the first step. My buddy Juggy lost 100lbs over the course of a year, quietly changing his diet and going to the gym. Once his changes became evident, half the crew was hitting him up for advice to get started.

Trying to change people won't accomplish much, and will probably result in damaged relationships. Focus on what you need to focus on, get help from others, and in turn help those who seek your help, but only if they're showing that they're also willing to help themselves.

"PEOPLE AREN'T PROJECTS, THEY'RE PEOPLE - AND LIKE IT OR NOT, THEY COME WITH FLAWS."

27 PAY THE COST

Everything and everyone has a price, and if we want things to happen, we have to prepared to pay the cost. That cost may be an hour of sleep, or our social lives, or our ability to keep up with pop culture. Whatever it is, the first step is to acknowledge that there will be a cost, and that in itself is more important to ensuring we achieve our goals.

We always encounter different types of people in our lives, and each of them is granted 24 hours in their day, but everyone is spending it differently. How we spend our time is how we spend our lives, and unfortunately, we can't do everything extremely well and at the same time. Like it or not — those sacrifices will need to be made. In order to make those sacrifices, we have to understand what those sacrifices will be. We have to recognize the costs, and make a down payment. That payment may be the pain at the gym, or strained relationship with our family. These types of costs are the reason so few people actually pursue the life they want. When they encounter resistance, they stop, and sometimes even turn around.

Nothing in life worth doing will be easy, or cheap. Love can be measured in action, and we have to be able to show ourselves how much something means to us, if we every really want to attain it. That can include leaving our ego at the door, letting down those around us, and not having an opportunity to live a traditional life.

Only we know what's important to us, and what we're willing to pay to get it, and what we're willing to lose to keep it.

"EVERYTHING AND EVERYONE HAS A PRICE, AND IF WE WANT THINGS TO HAPPEN, WE HAVE TO PREPARED TO PAY THE COST."

28 DADDY'S IPAD

Pops has just joined the world of internet within the past few months with his new iPad, and though it's great that he's broadening his horizons, he's also being exposed to a lot of fabricated news. After all, he's used to getting his news from trusted local reporters.

Coming from a culture where 'elders know best' it's very easy for outdated, and straight up incorrect information to continue to pass down from generation to generation.

One of the beautiful things about being human being is that our evolution is tied to the fact that we can build off the knowledge from those before us. With the internet, we can share knowledge almost instantly, and build upon it even quicker. But all things are double edged swords, and at the speed information can travel, misinformation is right behind it.

We're in an age of information, and it has value. People can benefit from spreading stuff around that may not be true, or a partial truth. That puts the responsibility on us to be critical of what comes our way, regardless of its source. Some information morphs over time, and meanings change, while some is manipulated purposely to serve the interests of specific individuals.

Critical thinking is key, and we have to question information passed on to us, whether it's been passed down for generations, or read yesterday off of Buzzfeed.

Question everything.

"CRITICAL THINKING IS KEY, AND WE HAVE TO QUESTION INFORMATION PASSED ON TO US, WHETHER IT'S BEEN PASSED DOWN FOR GENERATIONS, OR READ YESTERDAY OFF OF BUZZFEED."

29 THE OLDER I GET

The older I get, the less I think emotions will ever fully be understood, let alone controlled. Sometimes it feels like our mind is like a wild horse pulling every in every direction, and our days consist of simply holding on for dear life.

The more time I spend looking around, the less I feel like anyone really has things in the palm of their hand. Everyone is a bit scared, and many believe that they have it worse off than others, butt that's simply because we isolate ourselves from others, which amplifies what we're going through. When we're alone, these emotions echo.

Whether we prescribe to Disney movie love, or any other less romantic version of the idea, few of us can argue the impact those strong feelings have on our lives, and the way we live them out. We make up a battle between our heart and our mind, but that battle will always live in the brain.

Maybe the battle is necessary to help us sharpen our skills and teach us valuable lessons. Maybe the battles exist to weed out the strong from the weak. I don't know why they exist, I just know they do, and won't stop anytime soon, as we continue to blur the lines of what we want and what we need.

It's okay to feel the things we feel, they're a part of us, and can be more important than we think. It'll always be up to us to be open to wonderful things that may come with our challenges, struggles, and intense emotions.

"WE MAKE UP A BATTLE BETWEEN OUR HEART AND OUR MIND, BUT THAT BATTLE WILL ALWAYS LIVE IN THE BRAIN."

30 THE BEAUTY OF CONFUSION

One of the greatest disservices we can do to ourselves is actually believing that we've got it all figured out. We seem to have this need to want to figure everything out. But you know what? That's just not possible, and that's what can make life wonderful. The journey of discovery we can embark on, one that's focusing more on the questions than the answers, can take us further than we ever imagined. Life isn't a code to crack, it's an experience to have. Not having the answers will push us much farther on this journey, than believing we can know it all.

Not knowing can be scary, and we can easily lean towards following those who came before us, because they seemed to have a grasp on things. That's OK, to an extent, but as the world continues to evolve, we need to realize we need to evolve with it. The people from yesterday may not have everything we need to be prepared for tomorrow. Let's not simply follow the pattern of generations that came before us, but rather seek what they were seeking. Never stop questioning life in all aspects of it.

Life can be a beautiful journey of eternal discovery, if we allow it to be so.

Men never understand 'the woman', women never understand 'the man', therein lies the beauty of their being together. – Osho

"THE PEOPLE FROM YESTERDAY MAY NOT HAVE EVERYTHING WE NEED TO BE PREPARED FOR TOMORROW."

31 HERO TALK

I'm not sure who originally guilted me into thinking it was wrong to think about myself or put myself first. I understand greed, and I understand how self-indulgence might cause damage to the world as a whole, but there's something to be said when I have energy focused on myself, instead of having it concerned with the priorities of others.

Let's call it self-esteem, where our energy is leaning on the approval of others to simply exist. We need to be the hero in the book of our life in order to save ourselves from all the sh*t that we are surely to encounter.

Even if you're a believer of God, why not believe that you have been gifted and equipped with the necessary tools to overcome all the obstacles life puts in your way. Instead of praying to God to find the strength, pray to realize the strength you already have.

As an artist who was always, "Trying to keep it real," I rejected a lot of things that were necessary for my self-esteem because I thought it was too egotistical. The truth is, our ego is going to be our roommate regardless, and we need to figure out how to have a healthy relationship with it, instead of pushing everything away simply because we think it's too egotistical.

"If you're not the hero of your own novel, then what kind of novel is it? You need to do some heavy editing." – Terence McKenna

Don't believe in your hype, but believe in yourself, it's one of the most important thing you'll need to maneuver in this world.

"WE NEED TO BE THE HERO IN THE BOOK OF OUR LIFE IN ORDER TO SAVE OURSELVES FROM ALL THE SH*T THAT WE ARE SURELY TO ENCOUNTER."

32 WE GET WHAT WE WANT

If we pay attention long enough, we'll start noticing that people will actually get what they want most of the time. The biggest things to remember is that many of us are either unsure of what we want, or have mixed up what it really means to want something. Wanting a glass of water before bed is much different than wanting world peace. The first is a direct desire, that comes with a plan, that if executed will come true. The second is simply something that would be nice if happened on its own. If the things we want aren't accompanied with a plan and execution, then do we really want them?

Many people want to be rich, but not everyone is taking the necessary steps to make that a reality. Sitting at the same job day in and out hoping for the lottery numbers to match isn't an indication that someone wants to be rich, it's an indication that they wish it would happen. If we want something, we'll make it happen. There are people every day sacrificing things that many others wouldn't dream to give up, in order to make their wants a reality.

We all genuinely want different things, and we all eventually get them, but we have to be honest with ourselves about those wants. The best way to observe this is to see if the things we desire have an action plan behind them. Not knowing where to start, or waiting to be ready is simply an excuse. Richard Branson's Virgin Group empire (Virgin Airlines, Virgin Records, Virgin Mobile et cetera) was named in part from the idea that they were new to what they were doing and starting before they were ready.

What do you want from life? How bad do you want it? These questions can't be answered with words, only actions.

"IF THE THINGS WE WANT AREN'T ACCOMPANIED WITH A PLAN AND EXECUTION, THEN DO WE REALLY WANT THEM?"

33 TRINIDAD PART 1

In less than twenty-four hours, I'll be heading to Trinidad for the first time in my life.

When the shows were announced, I thought to myself, "Awesome, we get an all-expense paid trip to Trinidad, and after thirty shows, the 'work' part of this trip is second nature."

Thinking like that is why I don't have billboards of my face around the world.

Once Trinidad was announced, Lilly went into beast mode, redesigning much of the show just for the Trinidadian audience, that included flying in additional guest performers, an all new intro, closer and doubling the length of the music set.

This didn't need to happen, the show is amazing as it is, but Lilly doesn't want to kinda do well on any given night, she wants her to show to evolve and change as much as she does. And this was going to be a different beast.

There is no cutting of corners, no excuses, no searching for the path of least resistance. There's simply a vision, and an uncompromising commitment to follow through to make it happen.

After witnessing this level of hustle, work and commitment, it's very difficult for me to ever feel upset about my failures or lack of practice, because I have a front seat to witness what it takes to conquer the world. When you're working that hard, it's success or the dirt.

This mindset isn't for everyone, and neither Lilly or I are blind to the fact that there are a few jagged edges to this sword, but it is what it is.

I don't know what your potential is, but keep digging to find it, I've seen too far on the other side to turn around, I can promise you the journey will be an adventure of a life time. You can't fake the drive, some believe you can only be born with it, for my sake, I hope they're wrong. I'll continue to train and grind watching one of the hardest workers to ever do it.

But do me a favour: Don't tell Lilly I said all these nice things about her. I'll rip out the pages when I give her a copy of the book anyhow.

"YOU CAN'T FAKE THE DRIVE, SOME BELIEVE YOU CAN ONLY BE BORN WITH IT, FOR MY SAKE, I HOPE THEY'RE WRONG."

34 TRINIDAD PART 2

After an unnecessarily long journey to Trinidad, we arrive at the airport to fanfare I've never seen before. Sure we've had a lot of fans wait for us when we touch down, but to have every employee in the airport know who we were and what we're doing was a whole other experience.

We received a police escort out of the airport to a Trini-Chinese restaurant, where we had dinner (and almost lost one of our dancers, O'shani, to a fish allergy) after she was sent to the hospital, the rest of us were taken to our hotel and within an hour, we were already rehearsing. Since there were so many new elements added, plus a new dancer, a lot had to be reviewed. A few hours later, O'shani came back from the hospital, a bit weakened, but she was okay. We greeted her with hugs and lectures, because that's what family does.

The morning after we headed to the venue, which in itself was a sight to see. There were 5000+ seats placed across a giant convention centre, massive screens and ceiling fans, wires sprawled everywhere and massive speakers. This was the biggest show we had done to date.

The place was hot, the stage was wobbly, and time was not our friend. The next 24 hours was devoted to polishing all the tiny details that were getting overlooked. Whether it was getting props, finding safety pins, fixing up music edits, and arguing with the promoters last minute about security issues that could threaten the safety of the audience.

Yeah, it's a lot more complex than simply shaking our booties on stage.

Lilly had already begun losing her voice simply from having a meet and greet with fans the day before, and she had another 400 to meet on show day. We gave the show 140%, and it went off with many hitches (all shows do, it's just a matter of smiling through the mistakes) and the crowd's reception was nothing I was prepared for.

But all of that wasn't even the best highlight of the trip.

One of the special treats for the show was that Lilly brought out artists from the Island to perform on stage with her, the biggest being Machel Montano, the pride of Trinidad and a worldwide soca music phenomenon.

Not only was his presence a climax no one in the room could handle, he stayed behind to hang out with the crew after the show, and from conversations, we learned that he was much more than simply a talented singer with a knack for making catchy music. Machel turned out to be a monk in rockstar's clothing. He told us about his meditation excursions in India, and the bigger purpose of his work.

He invited us out to hang out a few days later. With only a handful of us left, we took him up on the opportunity, and we weren't disappointed.

We boarded a luxurious yacht, and the other guests on this outing were some of the most notable (and notorious) names on the island.

We danced, jumped into the Caribbean sea, and swam near an isolated island. It was a much-needed day off, and we chatted about everything under the sun.

Machel shared his beautiful views on life, and how he could mask a song about his love for God to easily pass for a love song for a girl. He talked about the responsibilities he felt as an influencer, and the art of creating things that are both enjoyable to experience, and contain substance for people to grow from.

We talked about life, power, corruption, celebrities, our dreams, our detractors, our supporters, our insecurities, our purposes, our loves, our losses, all while watching one of the most beautiful sunsets that can be seen on the planet.

We came home that evening to an intense work session. We were energized and given a whole new collection of WHYs for our work to continue.

Machel has been supporting himself since the age of twelve, he has grown into quite an artist and businessman, and the thing that struck me the most about him, or any other successful self-made individual, is their intense knowledge of self. They all look inside to understand, and help guide them for the decisions on the outside world.

I wish that was taught more in school.

"Bein' humble don't work as well as bein' aware." - Drake

We have to know ourselves better than we know anything else on this planet, it needs to be a lifelong journey of discovery, and it's going to require drowning out a lot of the noise the outside world is screaming at us.

No one can fully teach you how the world works, you can only discover it by discovering yourself. One great asset to help you on that journey is to surround yourself with people who are doing the same.

It's also no coincidence that you'll find many of these people as the most self-made successful people on the planet.

Thank you Trinidad, this experience was unforgettable, and only the first of many.

"NO ONE CAN FULLY TEACH YOU HOW THE WORLD WORKS, YOU CAN ONLY DISCOVER IT BY DISCOVERING YOURSELF."

35 MORE LESSONS WITH 50 CENT

It's common and normal to lean towards the path of least resistance. We want to get as much as possible out of a situation, while at the same time, putting in minimal effort. What we know, what's familiar, what scares us the least, will always be very appealing, but it isn't where we're going to find the growth we need.

We need to understand this in both ourselves, and those around us. 50 Cent eloquently put it, "People are loyal to their comfort." This is an extremely important reality to consider.

Trying to motivate yourself, or even a friend, to quit smoking, or to get out of an abusive relationship is going to come with resistance because we're challenging this fundamental principle. When it comes to approaching things beyond our comfort zone, there's going to be fear, and that's understandable. For this purpose we may be better off encouraging ourselves, and others, to tip toe out, rather taking a giant leap. Small changes are more doable, and will still add up in the long term. They'll also ensure that we ease out of our loyalties with our comfort rather than uncomfortably jerking ourselves out, priming us for relapses.

Not everyone equates happiness with growth, and not all growth will equate to happiness. Let's have honest dialogue with ourselves to see where our own loyalties lie. If we discover they are with our past, and the familiar, we can anticipate the fear that might come with moving forward. Awareness of this fear is very valuable, and will serve us well, as we continue to evolve.

"WHAT WE KNOW, WHAT'S FAMILIAR, WHAT SCARES US THE LEAST, WILL ALWAYS BE VERY APPEALING, BUT IT ISN'T WHERE WE'RE GOING TO FIND THE GROWTH WE NEED."

36 EXHAUSTED

We can exhaust our beings. If we spend time around people, or situations that require us to use extra calories just to put up with them, eventually, it's going to take a toll on us. Many people keep company that's not true to what they want and feel. A lot of us feel like we need masks to be around the people we spend time with, and whether that mask is a fake smile, or something to hide the real emotions underneath, it never does us any good long term. Doing this on a daily basis will suck us dry of our enthusiasm and energy towards life, and we can spiral into a less than pleasant human being.

The least flattering elements of our species can often come out when we don't feel that our needs are being met. This isn't exclusive to our basic needs for survival, it also includes things we need to keep our personal spirits fed and stimulated. If we spend the majority of our day around situations that don't allow for those needs, that can slowly chip away at us.

We can see this on reality TV, where people spend so much extra time trying to maintain some sort of composure on camera, that when they are exhausted, they lose it, and we get Drama.

We have to be mindful of the environments we put ourselves in. Are they providing us with energy, or simply causing it to deplete at a rate that is hard to replenish? Are the people we spend the most time with adding to our excitement for life, or simply leaving us exhausted?

I'm not advocating cutting everyone and everything off, that may not be realistic, but we always have control to possibly reduce the doses. We'll be better off ensuring that most of our days are spent in situations that feed us, not starve us.

"ARE THE PEOPLE WE SPEND THE MOST TIME WITH ADDING TO OUR EXCITEMENT FOR LIFE, OR SIMPLY LEAVING US EXHAUSTED?"

37 24 HOURS

I remember as a teacher, during a staff meeting, the principal had said something that really grinded my gears. I was upset, offended, annoyed, and wanted to lash out immediately. It was getting to the point where all I was seeing was red, and I was about to explode.

I told one of my colleagues about how livid I was, and how I was going to march into the Principal's office and give her a piece of my mind. He calmly sat me down, took his time to speak and said, "I know you're hurt and upset, and that's fine, but I think it's important you wait 24 hours before you say anything." I remember wondering why I would do that. He continued, "Just give it 24 hours, it won't hurt you to wait, and if after that time you still feel the need to say something, then by all means, go into her office and say it."

I took his advice, and low and behold, after 24 hours, the emotions were gone, and I really didn't feel like venting my frustrations anymore.

Our emotions can often get the best of us, and put us in situations where we speak before we're ready. The 24 hours I waited gave me time to put things in perspective and reevaluate if going ape-sh*t was really important or not. When other people do or say something that offends, hurts, or frustrates us, waiting 24 hours is a great way to ensure that not only are we not responding with emotions. It also ensures that we evaluate whether or not there's something else that's bothering us.

Maybe we're hungry, tired, or stressed from another situation, and that moment was a last straw that broke the camels back. Or maybe we are fully in our right to say something, and that additional 24 hours gives us time to organize our thoughts in words, so when we actually do approach the other person, we can be successful in getting our ideas across.

Since then, I've given myself the 24 hour rule, and often I don't even need 20 minutes before realizing that I shouldn't be sweating what ever is irking me. On those rare occasions where the clock runs out, and I still feel strongly about the situation, I'm confident and more prepared about how I'm going to approach it, and I'm more successful in resolving the problem.

If someone gets under your skin, give it 24 hours, not as a courtesy to them, but as a courtesy to yourself. That grace period can do wonders to improve any situation, and let us see clearly to whether addressing it is even worth our time.

Try it out.

"IF SOMEONE GETS UNDER YOUR SKIN, GIVE IT 24 HOURS, NOT AS A COURTESY TO THEM, BUT AS A COURTESY TO YOURSELF."

38 HACK AT THE UNESSENTIALS

Often times we feel like we need to build a life, or add to it, when really we should be doing the opposite. Instead of piling on more to our lives, we would be better off chipping away at the things that aren't important. Instead of focusing on a daily increase, let's focus on the decrease, then can we make room for the things that truly matter.

A journey of acquiring will also feel unfulfilled, especially if everything we're trying to attain comes from the outside world. Instead, let's focus on carving away the excess BS in our lives so we can get a better picture of who we are, and what's really important to the unique being we are.

Clarity comes from simplicity and simplicity requires us to have less around us. Too much of anything can often cause confusion, whether that's choices, ideas, things, and even people. Let's shed the stuff that isn't important and allow space for the essentials to flow through.

"TOO MUCH OF ANYTHING CAN OFTEN CAUSE CONFUSION, WHETHER THAT'S CHOICES, IDEAS, THINGS, AND EVEN PEOPLE."

39 AYAHUASCA

I remember taking a picture of my boarding pass when I was heading to Peru, and posting it online. I didn't tell my friends, my family found out the day before, and I only booked the ticket less than 2 weeks before.

One of the first comments on the picture was "Ayahuasca?". I showed my buddy Vlad, and we laughed out loud. Vlad works extensively in South America, and years prior I told him "If you're going to Peru, I want to come along" and his reply was the same, "Ayahuasca?".

He visited Peru about 4 times over those months, each time inviting me, and each time I had to say no. Either it was a financial issue, or I was already going to be somewhere else. But this time when he asked, October 2014, everything was aligned.

Ayahuasca is the root of death, and it's a cleansing experience done deep in the Amazon with the Inca people, some view it as a psychedelic drug, while others see it as a spiritual awakening. I was curious about it for years but like most things in my life, viewed it as a "maybe one day."

Instead one day came when a friend of mine returned from a trip to Peru and the first thing I asked him was "Ayahuasca?" he took me aside and spent 2 hours sharing his journey with me. His wife, who was with him, didn't participate in the ceremony, still said it was an enriching experience.

After that I figured if these responsible adults lived to talk about it, I should stop making excuses, and I found myself on a flight to Lima for a ten-day journey that would forever change me.

Ayahuasca contains the chemical DMT (N,N-Dimethyltryptamine) which is naturally produced in almost all living things on earth, including humans. We make DMT when we sleep, and it releases in our brain, and that influences our dreams. When we die, the brain is flooded with DMT, thus making our last moments alive both pleasant and very magical. In many cases, peopl had the flood of DMT in their brain. Taking Ayahuasca would be the experience of dying for about 5 hours.

Are you sold on it? No? Good.

I went into this experience with as little expectations possible, and was motivated to see what type of stuff was buried deep within me and how recognizing that could make me both more self aware, but also more comfortable in my own skin. Soldiers with Post Traumatic Stress Disorder, and other adults who have gone through their own trauma have found success using Ayahuasca to get to the bottom of their issues.

It's tricky to realize how much of our past experiences shape us, even when those experiences become distant and forgotten memories. The stress of getting lost at a department store as a child, can leave us with underlining feelings of abandonment that may follow us decades into the future, and we'll never know why.

I was excited to go through this process to see how far I could see under my hood.

We spent the night before purging ourselves of toxins by drinking fifteen very unpleasant cups of volcanic water. This went straight through us, and we spent most of the next few hours on the toilet shivering uncontrollably as our heart rates dropped, and volcanic water was coming out of every hole in our body.

Sold yet? No? Good.

We then took a twelve hour fast, and after a few hours of sleep in the hotel, took the journey towards the cabin into the Amazonian jungle. At this point, we were encouraged to take a vow of silence and focus only on what was happening to us on the inside. At the cabin is where we greeted our shaman, who would be performing the ceremony, as well as a nurse who would supervise.

Over the next few hours, all we were given to drink was cocoa leaf tea and water. We went through different practices and rituals. One that stood out most was that of forgiveness. We were encouraged to identify the people in our lives who we needed to forgive. I won't lie, that brought up some unpleasant emotions and memories, but what stood out most for me was when they asked us to focus on forgiveness towards ourselves.

I found myself even more consumed with emotions, thinking of all the things I needed to beg the universe to forgive me for. All the people I've mistreated, all the selfish decisions I made, all the lies I told.

I was fighting back tears, as we huddled up together for a group scream. You never realize how overdo you are to just scream your lungs out until you do it hugging other people who are doing the same.

I was given an individual tea leaf reading, in which the shaman would throw a handful of cocoa leafs in the air and read them as they landed on the ground. There was a junior shaman who spoke English translating the finding. The shaman spoke to me about everything from my relationship with the various people in my life, to my business affairs, to my health, and how it was all connected.

He told me to stop mutilating love.

He said I needed to stop telling others HOW to love me, and no longer allow them to dictate to me how I could love them. He connected some of the relationship troubles I had to a cold I had been carrying with me on my travels. His words did a lot to show me how dealing with my life on the outside affected the life I had within me. This isn't revolutionary, but when you're hearing it in the middle of the jungle from an Inca shaman who's reading leaves, it has a special impact.

Stop. Mutilating. Love. I'll never forget those words.

After my tea leaf reading, I was given another hour to lay in the sun and just reflect on what I experienced before the Ayahuasca ceremony would begin (yep, we haven't even gotten to the juicy stuff yet).

Although it seemed like these rituals and activities were taking a lifetime, it was only early afternoon by the time we were going to being the ceremony.

We sat in a large room, just Vlad and I, facing the two shaman and the nurse. She checked our blood pressure, recorded it, and said we were about to begin.

Then... We were given a sleeping bag, blankets and pillows, a giant bottle of water, toilet paper, and a bucket.

Sold yet? No? Still good.

Ayahuasca is a purge, and if you seen the movie, imagine that, but instead it's happening inside your body. Something was about to come in, and everything that no longer belonged was going to come out (hence the bucket and toilet paper).

It was funny because they spent some time instructing us on the ideal way to throw up into the bucket, none of that simple leaning over business, we had to go on all fours, hold the bucket like it was our lover, and embrace it.

Embracing these unpleasant experiences was a theme, and though we were warned that it may be a bumpy ride, we were heavily encouraged to focus on love, gratitude (or as they say with their accents gra-tee-toood), and happiness.

We were encouraged to thank God, Pacha Mama, the universe, or any other entities we felt connected with, and to recognize that the purge was going to be a good thing.

Most importantly we were told not to resist.
I'll never forget when the shaman said, "If you feel like you're going to die, then die, don't fight it."

This is the point where you realize you're in a cabin in the Amazonian jungle about to take the "root of death" while your family thinks your site-seeing.

Because I was vegetarian and Vlad wasn't, we were given two different mixtures and amounts of Ayahuasca. Our instructions were clear, we were not to vomit or lie down for the first 30 mins no matter what, but once the shaaman says it's OK to lie down, that also meant it was cool to begin purging as well.

The mixture was thick and not the tastiest thing I've ever had. I'm still shivering thinking it about it now, a year later. Imagine something as thick as chocolate syrup with roots and other goodness inside as you try to drink a whole glass.

As I sat there, trying not to throw up, I wondered if I made the right decision, there wasn't love and gratitude, there was fear of knowing that we can't go back now, and fear of the unknown.

What if it didn't work?
What if it worked too much?
What if we died, and they simply buried us somewhere in the jungle, never to be found?

I could feel my stomach bubbling, I began trying to take control of my breath.

As soon as the shaman gave us the go ahead, I jumped into position over my red bucket and began throwing up. The shaman rubbed my back, and blue smoke into my hair. He recited hymns, and reminded me "gra-tee-tood"

And that's when I saw the colours.

As I looked into bucket I was throwing up into, I started seeing swirls of colour, but wasn't as if the things in the bucket (mainly my vomit) were colourful. Instead it looked, and felt, like someone had peeled a layer from reality, and I could suddenly see what was happening underneath. The colours were flowing almost as if they were the layer of energy behind the scenes, with us at all times.

The closest visual I've seen to this is probably some of the stuff you see in the film Interstellar, odd shapes, textures and colours all moving non-stop.

I was also laughing my ass off as I was throwing up, screaming "Thank you mama, I'm good to go, thank you." Looking back at that, I think I was talking about dying.

I laid down and started enjoying the flow of colours that I was seeing, whether I kept my eyes closed or open. It was as if I could see the code in the Matrix, but it was much more beautiful. It wasn't just what I was seeing, I felt a part of it, one with it, I no longer felt like an individual drop, instead, I was a part of the vast ocean.

At one point, I saw a vision of a wolf, and he began speaking to me. Even before I could make out what he was saying, I thought to myself "Wow, this reminds me of that episode of The Simpsons when Homer ate the super hot pepper. Immediately that thought reshaped the realistic looking wolf into the wolf from the cartoon. I began to understand how my thoughts were shaping my visions. But the goal here wasn't control, my thoughts were polluting a natural journey, and for me to benefit fully, I would have to stop thinking (obviously that's easier said than done).

On top of all that, things were starting to get overwhelming.

I lay there with a smile tattooed to my face, repeatedly saying, "Thank you mama, I'm good to go." The colours got brighter, the pain in my stomach got more intense (after all I had been dry heaving at this point after a few rounds of vomiting), and the speed of the flowing colours was faster than a rollercoaster.

I felt dizzy, I wanted to throw up, but nothing came out, I opened my eyes to see what was in my bucket, it was dark slime. I got frightened, so I signalled for the nurse for help.

She came and held my hand, and I told her, "Okay I'm done, I get it, but it's too overwhelming, give me something to go to sleep. I'm over this. How much time is left?"

At this point it had only been 45 minutes, the average Ayahuasca trip lasts 5 hours.

F*ck. Me.

The nurse, who herself had multiple experiences with the plant, told me to relax, and to focus on love, and that I would be fine, and not to fight it. I kept replying "Naw, just give me some NyQuil, let me go to sleep, I'm over this." She told me to relax, drink some water and lie down.

As I lay down, I started seeing faces, random faces. I saw an Italian Opera Clown, he looked back at me and shrugged. I saw a kid riding an ice cream bike, I saw a gang of other random faces, none which I recognized, none which were particularly unique. It was as if I was walking down any random street staring at people walking by. The only thing I noticed was that we all made eye contact. Part of me felt this was a journey of confidence, as avoiding eye contact is something we all do with strangers. There really wasn't an opportunity to look away from them, anyhow.

The stomach pains became more intense, the colours were changing quickly, and I was feeling more disoriented. The room we were in became darker, and I felt like a child in a nightmare. I could hear Vlad throwing up, and that made me even more uncomfortable.

I asked to go outside, see the sun, see nature. The Shaman and nurse that I should remain indoors. I told them I needed to go to the bathroom, and then ran outside anyway.

The Jr. shaman followed me out, and kept his arm around me, he asked me to go back inside, and I explained that things were too intense, and that I needed a more peaceful environment. What he said next changed everything.

He said, "I'll let you spend five more minutes outside, then we're going back inside. This journey isn't about the outside world, it's about the world inside you. Right now by having your eyes open, and trying to distract yourself with everything out here, you're avoiding everything you should be paying attention to on this journey. I need you to go back inside, and I need you to look within, and face everything, and learn from it."

It made sense, I was running away, even though I signed up for a few hours of discomfort, I didn't anticipate things being as uncomfortable as they were. I used the bathroom one more time, slowly went back upstairs, went into the room and headed for my makeshift bed.

I stared at Vlad for the first time, He's Chilean with wavy hair and a small beard, his eyes were half open, as well as his mouth, he looked dead, but at peace. He looked more like a fallen Iraqi soldier than my homeboy on a psychedelic trip.

As I lay down, I closed my eyes, and decided to think a happy thought. The first thought that came to my mind was "mama" but this time I wasn't thinking of the universe, or Pacha Mama, I thought of my mother. I imagined her face, and immediately felt warmth in my body, and a smile on my face. I began to have calmer visions of sunsets and water, the colours were beautiful and things felt more peaceful. Memories of the shaman reminding me not to mutilate love echoed in my ears. The colours got weaker, I realized that things weren't necessarily getting under my control, but rather things were wearing off.

I untied my turban, and retied it to cover my eyes, but all I saw was black. The colours were gone and the room no longer felt anything more than a room. It didn't feel like things simply wore off, it felt as if I was abandoned, as if Pacha Mama decided that I was a child throwing a fit, and the best thing to do was walk away.

I desperately clutched my eyes closed, hoping for colours to spill out, but there was nothing. It was over as soon as it began.
Did I survive the journey? Well I think those bathroom breaks flushed out a lot of the root. Was it a spiritual experience? I feel like it was more psychedlic than spiritual, but it did take me deep into myself and brought out many of my insecurities and discomforts. There were a lot of ideas that stayed with me from the experience.

But would I go back? Not anytime soon, maybe in ten years, and I would spend a few weeks beforehand cleaning myself out and putting myself in a better situation to deal with the physical toll of the experiences.

Was it worth it?

Most definitely. It was a fear to overcome, and a check on the bucket list, I was given an opportunity to visit a layer beneath the self I had trouble seeing in the first place.

Would I recommend it others?

It's definitely not for everyone, and many of the places people go to conduct the ceremony are neither as safe, or reliable as the place I went to, which came with a heavy price tag. The changes that came from the experience were permanent; this wasn't simply a case of getting high on a drink and watching it wear off. Doors were open that haven't closed, and memories were made that will never be forgotten.

The next day I was in the bathroom of the hotel, staring at the designs on the tiles, and I began having flashbacks of my visions. As I mentioned before, many of the visuals are similar to those in Interstellar, I watched the movie after this experience, and the flashbacks were very vivid.

I don't think drinking Ayahuasca took me to a new magical dimension, but it definitely allowed my brain to make new connections, and give me insights into what my mind is capable. At times, I felt superiorly enlightened, and at others, I began to think I was schizophrenic, and imagined this is how the average individual with a mental illness may feel on a daily basis.

At the end of the day the mind works best open, like all choices in life, Ayahuasca has its consequences, both good and bad.

If you take this route, please do be safe, there have been reported deaths, and many of the ceremonies are happening in places where you don't have access to medical facilities.

Most of my family found out AFTER the fact, and many more will only learn about it after reading this chapter.

I can't define spirituality, nor do I know if I prescribe to things that are considered purely spiritual. Taking Ayahuasca was my attempt to see if I needed to figure out the difference, it helped me realize that I don't.

"We are not human beings having a spiritual experience. We are spiritual beings having a human experience."

- Pierre Teilhard de Chardin

"I CAN'T DEFINE I KNOW IF I PRESCRIBE CONSIDERED PURELY

TAKING AYAHUASCA TO SEE IF I NEEDED DIFFERENCE, IT HELPED DON'T."

SPIRITUALITY, NOR DO
TO THINGS THAT ARE
SPIRITUAL.

WAS MY ATTEMPT TO
FIGURE OUT THE
ME REALIZE THAT I

40 SHAME

I realized that growing up in a house where religion had woven itself into the moral fiber of the house that the moral police wasn't God, it was people. Their laws were based on what they understood (or wanted to understand) and instead of guns and batons, they used guilt and shame to punish anyone they those committed crimes.

This tactic isn't reserved exclusively for the religious. Anyone with a strong belief in anything (hi there, PETA) can use the same tactics.

Shame is like that imaginary electronic fence that tells our imaginary dog collars to shock us if we cross some imaginary limits. We don't test them often, and people that don't seem concerned with the opinion are often described as having, "No shame". Ideas like shame and guilt are abstract, and can differ significantly depending on where we are in the world. Some things seem innate (like using the bathroom in public) while others seem socialized (like fashion choices).

Shame has been used as weapon for a very long time. It can immobilize us and make us conscious that other people may be paying attention. We then become prisoners of our reputations, and those self-imposed fences are very hard to climb over.

Often the people around us help to build those fences, as it helps to reinforce their own fears and insecurities. Worrying about what people think can be an infinitely stressful and paralyzing thought, and much of that does well to keep us standing still.

Shame is often taught, and if we spend time recognizing how shame is used to keep us in line, we've taken the first step to liberating ourselves from it. Don't let people shame you into submission and don't let society, religion or any other socialized structure hold you hostage simply because they don't deem what you want to be worthy.

Surround yourself with open-minded people who are much more curious than judgmental. They'll allow you to be who you want to be, and that will most definitely make life feel a lot lighter.

"SURROUND YOURSELF WITH OPEN-MINDED PEOPLE WHO ARE MUCH MORE CURIOUS THAN JUDGMENTAL."

41 SUICIDE

It's a heavier thought than we want to admit when we start to think about ending our own existence. But I think we can be honest with each other, it happens far more often than anyone wants to admit. I've had dark times, and when I felt like I couldn't see light at the end of the tunnel, I had thoughts about what I could take to go to sleep and never wake up. There's a despair that many of us have inside of us, that we struggle to communicate with the world around us. Maybe we're embarrassed or ashamed, or terrified that if we spoke out, no one would care.

Imagine we told someone we wanted to end our life, and they didn't care. That's such a horrifying thought.

We may not think the suicide hotlines are for us, we may have already given ourselves the pep talks, and clichéd reasons to appreciate life, and maybe none of that has worked.

Sometimes life itself has to change drastically for the better for us to get out of our funk. Maybe a turn in fortune is important, before we can muster up the courage to keep on moving.

Clinging on to hope seems useless when hope is this hollow idea that slowly fades away as the days go by and we don't see any improvement.

I've been there, and to be honest, I may find myself back there again, as scary as that may be. We all have our own level strengths and our own breaking points, and a simple twist of fate can easily get me back to contemplating my own demise once more.

But I can say that time is your friend, and although it's hard stick something out when we want these feelings to stop, we can still busy ourselves seeking help from those who know how to give it.

Suicide is a final option, and there are literally hundreds of other options to explore before making such a permanent decision. It's one thing we can't reverse, repent, or repair.

Create that light in the tunnel. Fight for every moment you have been blessed with. Realize the biggest lie you are telling yourself is, "things can't get better." You know what? Things can most definitely get better, as long as we devote ourselves to making it happen and sticking to it for months and even years, because fighting for our own existence is the most important thing we can ever do.

Seek help, your thoughts and feelings are common and normal, there are people out there who can put the right words together far better than I can. I'm here to encourage you to get the help, because I got help and I see the world through a different lense. Life feels much better now than it ever has.

A lot of those things are attributed to time. Time does the healing, just not on our schedule. Stick it out get the help you deserve, and remember that your life is worth fighting for.

"SUICIDE IS A FINAL OPTION...
IT'S ONE THING WE CAN'T REVERSE,
REPENT, OR REPAIR."

42 COURAGE

Courage isn't a lack of fear, it's feeling scared, but moving forward regardless. Our fears can serve as a compass to point us towards the things and places we should be heading towards. Having courage simply means we're aware of the fear, but don't allow it to paralyze us in life. Courage is feeling the fear, but doing the thing that scares us anyway.

We'll often talk ourselves out of things because of fear. This is normal, so don't feel like a coward because of it. What needs to shift is the type of attention we're giving our fear. As animals we have instincts meant to keep it out of harms way, and modern day fear-mongering has jumbled those instincts. These days, a lot of the things we fear aren't actually associated with actual harm.

In this modern world, our fears are the fences that ensure we remain in our comfort zones. It can be anything from making excuses to procrastinating, to outright running away from our problems. We admire others who don't seem to have these fears, but we need to realize they probably do, but they move ahead regardless.

When we overcome what we fear the most, the fear conquered becomes a strength acquired, and one of the best ways to begin this conquest is with baby steps.

Sometimes the bravest thing we can do is to simply admit we're scared. That tiny step in itself is the first thing we need to do to conquer what's in front of us.

"SOMETIMES THE BRAVEST THING WE CAN DO IS TO SIMPLY ADMIT WE'RE SCARED."

43 HUMBLE THE HEDGEHOG

Relationships. I'm not too good at that sh*t.

That should be the whole chapter there. Full stop.

There's something called the hedgehog dilemma, where hedgehogs have trouble getting close together in order share body heat because of their sharp spikes. Some of us seem to have that same dilemma - we can't find the right amount of space between others and ourselves. If we get too close, we get hurt and if we're too far apart we'll drift. This happy medium sounds like something out of a fairytale. You hear about it all the time, but still don't believe it's true.

We all want to be close to others in some capacity, and we want some type of reciprocity (that's a big word for receiving back what we put out). The challenge is figuring how much distance we need between the people we have these relationships with. Some of the people in our lives need to be attached to us at the hip, while others need to be far away and infrequently involved in our lives. The dose of these people will vary depending on the situation.

It doesn't bother me that I'm a hedgehog, the experience of having relationships with people is exploration for me. I'm not sure there's a specific code to crack here, more than simply a crack to discover in our own foundation. Maybe the solution for some is to devote less time to their relationships, while for others it would be the opposite.

As someone who promotes leaving their own comfort zones, and not taking the safe route, there's still something to be said about taking time to let wounds heal if you have them, and busying yourself with other things in the meantime. Even as adults, we hold on to pain that we experienced as kids, and addressing that pain can determine and motivate the choices we make.

I've been stabbed by a few spikes, and I most definitely stabbed a few other would-be hedgehogs in my life, and I think now devoting myself to other things isn't because I don't want to try with people anymore, but rather because I still need more time.

Only you know the real reasons you do certain things in your life. It's solely our responsibility to set the doses for the people we let in. It may take a little trial and error, but even recognizing that getting too close might be an issue, can save a few spikes stuck in the skin.

"SOME OF THE PEOPLE IN OUR LIVES NEED TO BE ATTACHED TO US AT THE HIP, WHILE OTHERS NEED TO BE FAR AWAY AND INFREQUENTLY INVOLVED IN OUR LIVES. THE DOSE OF THESE PEOPLE WILL VARY DEPENDING ON THE SITUATION."

44
UNSIGNED PERMISSION SLIPS

Maybe if I accomplish more they'll accept me, maybe if I have more followers online, they'll respect me. Maybe if I have a six-pack. Maybe if I made more money, found a pretty girl, made it on the TV shows with the white people, I'll gain more acceptance.

Maybe if I do everything except be myself, they'll accept me.

They won't accept us, because there is no 'they.'

We have to stop waiting for the world to grant us permission to be ourselves, or anyone else for that matter, because that's not how things work. Even though we long for that acceptance, there's no one on the other line. I have a chip on my shoulder that I'm trying to address. Every moment of rejection I encountered in life plays back in my head, as I hope the next milestone will be a giant "take that" to the invisible audience of people that hurt me.

The truth is, the people that hurt me in the past are victims themselves, and they're walking around chasing their own happiness. The kids that teased me were just kids. Most of them probably don't remember the things they said or did to harm me, and that reminds me that I may have done the same.

"The axe forgets, the tree remembers." – African proverb

There won't be a big moment of triumph where we'll feel we officially belong. There's no one to sign these permission forms that grant us the freedom to relax and let our guard down. There isn't even anyone to check to make sure we got the right kind of permission. There's only us. We have to remind ourselves, that it's okay to be who we are, and that the needs to be accepted by others is very real, but isn't a thirst so easily quenched.

Instead of starting to gain acceptance from the world around us, let's instead focus accepting the world that exists within us. Once we're more comfortable in our own skin, what anyone else thinks becomes less relevant to our happiness and well-being.

Stop trying to get permission to be who you are going to be, there's not one to sign it, and no one to check it. You can be who you want to be, the moment you allow yourself to do so.

"WE HAVE TO STOP WAITING FOR THE WORLD TO GRANT US PERMISSION TO BE OURSELVES..."

45 LET'S TALK ABOUT SEX BABY

Growing up it almost felt like girls were forbidden until the day they were no longer forbidden. I remember a life where talking to any girl seemed to be punishable by death, and then everything changed. I was getting ready for a university party and my sister mentions to my mother that there would be many girls present. My eyes widened expecting my mother to give me a long lecture and warning about going, but instead she said, "…And that's what you're going to wear? Don't you have anything nicer?"

There are protests in the city of Toronto over sex education. Some parents fear a curriculum that encourages children to be more aware of their bodies is going to lead to more promiscuous behavior, and that the best way to prepare children for such topics is to say nothing at all. The reality is, if the responsible entities in our lives don't expose us to a responsible way of looking at things like sex, then our youth is going to be left to their own devices. I went to a junior high school that had pregnant students at thirteen, and classmates that still didn't even understand where babies came from. That, truthfully, is the real danger.

People can be uninformed, misinformed, or simply biased, and all three of those in relation to sex education can have some disastrous consequences. I completely understand the fear that comes with bringing such a topic up, but saying less will actually do more damage than saying more at this time in a kid's life.

These protests can get pretty loud, and my 9-year-old nephew asked my sister one day, "What's sex?" Because that's not something that would not have been taught to him in the education system for another two years. It's the Barbara Streisand effect all over again.

Open communication isn't easy. It's downright awkward, especially when we're talking about topics that are considered taboo, but that doesn't mean it isn't important to do so. Censorship never works, and that's not an opinion, so let's not set ourselves up for failure. Hiding information will only hurt those who need it the most.

Sex is complicated; it involves emotions, feelings, psychology and everything else under the sun. It's at the center of a lot of art, and is used to sell products. It's one of the most interesting phenomena that connect us to the rest of this animal planet. No matter how intelligent we think we are, mother nature still pulls the strings and has put in us urges that drag us along and dictate a lot of our life decisions.

Whether you're a parent reading this wondering how to have this conversation with your child, or a young'n frozen with fear at the idea of ever mentioning the word SEX to your parents, realize it's only as harmful as we make it. It's okay to talk, and to not prevent others from being able to listen.

"PEOPLE CAN BE UNINFORMED, MISINFORMED, OR SIMPLY BIASED, AND ALL THREE OF THOSE IN RELATION TO SEX EDUCATION CAN HAVE SOME DISASTROUS CONSEQUENCES."

46 LOOKS DON'T MATTER, PRESENTATION DOES

I'm not going to tell you looks don't matter, and idealistically say that we're all beautiful on the inside, and that's all that's important. That would be too idealistic of me and the truth is, we're visual animals, that collect and process a lot of information that arrives through our eyes. So what does that mean? It means that what is seen is very important, but that doesn't necessarily mean our looks are a part of it.

Smiles make the best make up, whether teeth are showing or not. We can all benefit from sharing ours with the world much more. In terms of how we look, we have to remember that comparing our appearance to that which is promoted in media is irrelevant. Different people find different things attractive. Some girls dig beards, while others don't, that's life (and cue my sadness). But at the end of the day, we shouldn't focus on our looks for the approval of others, because there are too many 'others' to impress, instead we can work on our appearance and presentation in the way that allows us to feel confident about sharing ourselves with the world.

We don't have to wear expensive clothes, but we shouldn't be ignorant to the fact that fashion choices can make a difference. We can find styles we like, and then emulate them. Fashion is art, and a fun art at that. Not everything has to be couture, or ridiculously expensive. Trends can change too quickly for people to spend excessive amounts of money on articles of clothing that will spend next year in the back of the closet.

How we present ourselves is also a reflection of our efforts and care towards who we are. The best accessories we can wear every day are still going to be a smile, and great posture. Let's do it so we can be excited to look in the mirror. Confidence is the most attractive thing we can project.

"THE BEST ACCESSORIES WE CAN WEAR EVERY DAY ARE STILL GOING TO BE A SMILE, AND GREAT POSTURE."

47 I THREW A STONE AT GOD

It's interesting relationship, the one we have with God. God gets all the credit when things go well, and next to none of the blame when sh*t hits the fan. Ask ten people about God, and you'll of course get ten different stories. For some God is a supreme being with characteristics of a human being, their God can become jealous, angry, happy, and vengeful, and if you don't stay on God's good side, be prepared for an unpleasant life.

For others God can simply be the collection of energy that exists in this universe, kind of like the ocean, once we put all the drops together. Rumi says, "We are drops in the ocean, and an ocean in a drop," and that can almost be seen as a prophecy for the Internet, in a way. The one giant global brain we're becoming.

When I was young, I was aggressively encouraged and bribed into memorizing the pronunciations of hymns in old Punjabi, though rarely understanding what I was saying, I would present it well, much to the delight of the adults. As a teenager, I used to have conversations with God everyday, as I walked my dog. I used to give thanks, and ask for forgiveness. God was an absentee father who my mother would force me to write letters to, I only knew of him through stories, but I was assured he knew me better than I knew myself. That didn't encourage me to become more self aware, that simply frightened me.

I didn't know what was right and what was wrong, I didn't know about some of the thoughts and feelings I was having, and if they were acceptable to God. I only knew I couldn't hide from him.

Always a him for some reason, except in Peru, they called her Pacha Mama

Then sometimes someone would frame god as all-loving, and that we were all his children, and he loved us all equally, that included the Hitlers, the rapists, and the people who double-dip in the salsa bowl. That would make me feel a bit easy, because surely I was better than those monsters, but at the same time, it still confused me as to why those monsters existed in the first place.

"It's a test from God," or my favourite, "God works in mysterious ways." Or even, "Stop asking so many questions." I turned to the scriptures in Sikh philosophy and realized that many of the same types of questions were being asked more than answered. And often when praise of "God" was being given it was simply a reference to the self. As I got older, a friend showed me how the "you" could simply be a reference to the truth, whatever that may be.

I'm not a flaming atheist, you know the types that are so butt-hurt from being force fed any concept of God, that they know have made it their life's mission to disprove his existence, not to mention show that religion is nothing but detrimental to the world. Nor, I should point out, am I a theist, or agnostic, or any other of the labels folks have so proudly adopted because it seems to be important to have a say in the conversation. I'm simply a listener.

I want to continue to appreciate and show gratitude, but that doesn't often have a specific direction. I don't fear judgment, and I'm living as if once my lights go out, they go out. Energy cannot be created or destroyed, so once I'm dead, my energy will just be redistributed amongst the universe of which I'm already a part.

I don't think about heaven or hell, both the world around me, and within me, show pieces of both concepts. There isn't an argument here for me. Even with steady improving living conditions for the average human being, around sixteen thousand children die every day from preventable causes. If there really is a supernatural entity up there that I'm going to have to answer to when it's my time, better believe I'll have some heavy questions of my own.

I've seen both the beauty and black eye that ideas of God have blessed the world, I can't say either is better than the other, but I know the power of belief has done some extraordinary things, and we should never view it lightly. I threw a stone at God, She smiled from her throne and let it fall… Like her favourite angel.

"...THE POWER OF BELIEF HAS DONE SOME EXTRAORDINARY THINGS, AND WE SHOULD NEVER VIEW IT LIGHTLY."

48 HEADS OUT OF THE CLOUDS

The difference between a dream and a goal is a plan. The problem is that sometimes our "plans" simply consist of hoping that everything will work itself out.

Instead of daydreaming and becoming lost in the world of fantasy, we can use these moments to strengthen our relationship with reality. There's nothing wrong with wanting to aspire to great things, even things that haven't been accomplished before. Where the danger lies, is if we find ourselves wishing and hoping our days away.

What we will be better off doing is tougher. When we find ourselves daydreaming and fantasizing, let's remind ourselves of our present circumstances, not to discourage ourselves, but rather, to help to create a mental road map of where we are at the present time to where we want to be in the future.

If we're dreaming of six figures in our bank account, let's bring the focus back to our reality (and how much money we have), and we can ask ourselves the honest question of, "How do I get there from where I am now?"

Creating such a pathway mentally is one of the first steps on planning and executing the journey towards that goal. If we find ourselves saying, "I don't know," when constructing this map, then let's focus on the first few steps that can be identified, and reevaluate from there.

There is no need to keep our heads in the clouds and cross our fingers that things will work out. We are the architects, designers and construction workers of the life we want. Let's begin sketching out the blueprint.

The most important step for that is to continually bring ourselves to reality so where know where to start.

As always, though it's great to have goals, the journey is the most important part, so work to enjoy it every step of the way.

"WE ARE THE ARCHITECTS, DESIGNERS AND CONSTRUCTION WORKERS OF THE LIFE WE WANT. LET'S BEGIN SKETCHING OUT THE BLUEPRINT."

49 COMMITMENT VS. INVOLVEMENT

When I was a teacher, my reputation wasn't that of a hard-worker. If anything I was seen as the opposite, but it seemed to be excused because of my age, and the fact that I got along with most of the staff in the school. It was odd that at the same time, in my circles in the art world, I was known for having a monstrous work ethic. It even confused me at the time. How can someone be so lazy at one thing, and so committed to another? Aren't lazy people lazy all the time, and hard-workers working hard at everything? Apparently not.

I wasn't committed to my job as a teacher. I was simply involved in it. Kind of like a relationship. It wasn't my first love, but it made the most sense to stay in it, because it provided me many of the things I thought were important at the time. Meanwhile, Humble the Poet wasn't earning enough to even cover my phone bill, but the sleepless nights and endless amounts of effort came naturally to make sure I hustled.

Let's not get it twisted, as we fast forward to present day, sometimes I find myself wondering how it felt so seamless back then. Maybe it was knowing that I had a paycheck coming in regularly. Maybe I wasn't fully committed to anything besides having fun with the art and stroking my ego.

But now things have evolved, the stakes are higher because this is my life and livelihood. I feel like my level of commitment is higher than it's ever been, because I don't see myself turning around for anything. It's this or the dirt. So what are you commitments? I'm asking about the things that never leave your mind. The ideas you obsess over, the ones that make time stand still. What is that thing in your life that you are more than simply involved in?

"The difference between involvement and commitment is like an eggs-and-ham breakfast. The chicken was involved but the pig was committed." - Anon

"AREN'T LAZY PEOPLE LAZY ALL THE TIME, AND HARD-WORKERS WORKING HARD AT EVERYTHING? APPARENTLY NOT."

50 PRIORITIES

One of the greatest gifts we can give ourselves is the awareness of what's truly important in our lives. Our priorities are what consciously and unconsciously guide us, but many people never take the time to fully discover what those may be to them. It's common for us to look at those around us, and begin using their stories as a basis for writing our own. If everyone is going to school, getting a job, getting married, and having kids, it's completely normal for us to feel that we may be bound to those same trajectories. At this point keeping up with everyone else may become a priority, whether that squares with who we are as a person or not.

We're unique creatures, and sometimes what may be good for one, may not be the best for another. If we enjoy quiet nights while everyone else is out partying, that's okay. We're better off simply for knowing exactly what makes us smile. When we know our priorities, we can communicate them to those we have relationships with. Successful relationships are often a result of priorities that align, so the first step is to know what those priorities are.

Discovering our priorities generally requires a journey within. The rest of the world can only teach us through the way we react to in internally. If we're not paying attention to our thoughts, feelings, and emotions, we may never discover the things that are important to us.

What's really important to you? What agrees with your being? Start digging inside to find out what those are, so it can serve as a guide for the life you want to live.

"IF WE'RE NOT PAYING ATTENTION TO OUR THOUGHTS, FEELINGS, AND EMOTIONS, WE MAY NEVER DISCOVER THE THINGS THAT ARE IMPORTANT TO US."

51 YOU KNOW NOTHING HUMBLE PO

Some of the dumbest points in my life all had to do with times I felt I knew it all. Being sure of yourself is one thing, being sure of the truth, as it relates to the rest of the universe is a whole other ball game. Thinking I understood how things worked in the world, even though I barely had a few decades on it, set me up for many disasters. As they say, we learn best the hard way, and learn I did.

The danger of thinking we have all the answer is that we're then closing ourselves off to the important questions, and possible new knowledge.

The confusion and complexity of life makes it attractive to lean towards people or ideas that have it all figured out, but beware. Nobody has it all figured out.

If you believe in a higher power, than put some faith that the almighty equipped you with the tools and learning ability to maneuver in this world. If you don't look at life that way, then just remember to keep your heart and mind always open to new things, because we discovering new and amazing things all the time.

There's an appeal to people who claim to know it all, and that's the reason they're so dangerous, to both themselves and others. Many people who claim to know it all, and will share it for a one-time fee, probably don't believe in what they're selling, but they know others will.

And if anyone claims to have all the answers, run as far away from them as quickly as possible.

"SOME OF THE DUMBEST POINTS IN MY LIFE ALL HAD TO DO WITH TIMES I FELT I KNEW IT ALL."

52 F*CK YOUR RIGHTS

Entitlements are not your friend. We often talk about our rights to things; happiness, freedom, love, the rights to be ourselves, but where did all this thinking of rights come from?

In no way am I advocating that we strip people of their rights. Rather, I'm encouraging us to remember that rights can breed entitlements, and entitlements breed unrealistic expectations.

Depending on where you are in the world right now, the rights you have differ from people in other regions. We all have to work within the environments we're in and understand the terrain we're walking on. Having expectations that someone else will ensure we get what we want will most definitely lead to disappointment.

We're better off not having entitlements and appreciating the freedoms we have. The moment they become what we already expect, we might lack the gratitude necessary to enjoy them. That will also set us up for a lot of discomfort if they are stripped away (and if you read a little history from any culture, you'll realize how easily this can happen).

Let us not take things for granted. It doesn't matter if it's access to clean, drinkable water, or the ability to actually have free speech, these are privileges that aren't afforded to many of our fellow humans around the world. I use the word privilege because we're lucky to have them, and we can lose them at any moment.

"IN NO WAY AM I ADVOCATING THAT WE STRIP PEOPLE OF THEIR RIGHTS. RATHER, I'M ENCOURAGING US TO REMEMBER THAT RIGHTS CAN BREED ENTITLEMENTS, AND ENTITLEMENTS BREED UNREALISTIC EXPECTATIONS."

53 POORA

My father's mother, my grandmother, I called her Biji. Her name was Giaan Kaur, such a beautiful name. She was under five feet tall, but resilient and feisty. I was a child of her eldest son, so I was given preferential treatment. She was sweet to me, spoiled me, would cook me French fries in the toaster oven because she didn't know how to use the big one on the stove.

When I was 12, I remember walking with her to the convenience store to buy some milk. I vividly remember her saying "I'm waiting for you to get married, so I can die". I laughed and said, "you're not allowed to die until my kids get married." She laughed and that was the deal.

In 2008, I came home from a late night hanging out with friends, and the lights were still on in the house. Right before I got to the door, my cousin called me to say that Biji had passed away. She was in India with my Papa Ji at the time. I walked in to see my parents sitting in the family room. My father looked at me and, in Punjabi, said that Biji had become Poora.

Poora means complete, or full, depending on how you use it. What an interesting way to describe death.

My grandmother wasn't dead; she was complete. Like the credits had begun to roll in the film of her life.

Also she was the healthiest of my grandparents, she was the first to. In their village in Rajasthan, She made my Papa Ji breakfast, and went to lay down after. When he went in to check on her, she was gone.

There wasn't a funeral, not all of my father's siblings were allowed to fly to India for a final viewing. I couldn't imagine losing my mother, and being told that there was no point in flying to see her because she'll be cremated before you get there. Around the world there are different definitions of death, and different definitions of grieving. In this case, there was simply a call from my grandfather saying, "Biji was poora."

I thought of the promise we made to each other, how my children would be married before she passed. Meanwhile, I'm no closer to getting married myself. But my life is not lived for her, and her life isn't lived for me, we both have our own journeys until we become complete.

All of our credits will roll one day, and we too will become complete. Will we feel complete when that time comes? Well, that depends on the life we decide to live while we're here.

"POORA MEANS COMPLETE, OR FULL, DEPENDING ON HOW YOU USE IT. WHAT AN INTERESTING WAY TO DESCRIBE DEATH."

54 MILLION MILES A MINUTE

My mind, like many of yours, is this machine that seems to have the random switch on, and it shoots the most obscure and unrelated thoughts into my head at a rate of a million thoughts a minute.

Some of these thoughts are so marvelous and so genius that I find myself in awe of them, but by the time I try to get pen to paper (or fingers to keyboard) they wither away. I talked myself out of the idea I had in my head for whatever reason. I only recently realized that maybe it was the execution of the ideas that was the roadblock.

I couldn't focus on one idea at a time. I mean, I still can't focus on one idea at a time, but at least I know that's something I have to work on.

Staying focused and in the present is a skill worth practicing. So many of the world's most successful people attribute focus as the biggest factor to their output. It's interesting though, because focus can also include having severe tunnel vision. When you're so focused on one thing, nothing else is allowed to come in. That's wonderful in the sense that it drains out distractions, but it can also keep us blind to the changes happening around us. We can focus on a goal, but be flexible with our plans.

So instead of dollar signs on my vision board, I have a picture of a man meditating. Maybe meditation is the answer, and at the same time, maybe I have to make peace with the storm that exists around me. Every once in a while I catch something so amazing that focus becomes easier.

"WE CAN FOCUS ON A GOAL,
BUT BE FLEXIBLE WITH OUR PLANS."

55 F*CK YO CELL PHONE

It always annoyed me to see that my cell phone company was giving out better plans to new customers, while I, a loyal customer of many years, pays standard rate. I'd have to call in, spend 20 min belly aching about this before I'd receive a blue tooth earpiece in the mail; I don't even use the stupid thing.

That's how so many of our relationships have become. We neglect the situations that require the least maintenance, to focus on newer ones.

If you don't feel that this applies to you, then please stick around anyways, so I don't feel like I'm the only here.

Let's shift the mindset to reward loyalty, and only allow ourselves to be in the relationships that treat us the same.

In a temporary world, it means something to know that someone wants to spend their temporary time you. Whether that's a good friend, lover, co-worker or drug dealer (I just wrote that to make sure you were paying attention, or did I), loyalty means something. Don't allow anyone to set the standards of a relationship lower than the ones you want for yourself. Lowering yourself to the standards of others is suffocating yourself in the cocoon. Be around people that allow, and encourage you to be yourself, those people are gifts and deserve to be reminded of that.

Like a neglected friend, I left my old cell phone company for someone who will treat me right.

"LET'S SHIFT THE MINDSET TO REWARD LOYALTY, AND ONLY ALLOW OURSELVES TO BE IN THE RELATIONSHIPS THAT TREAT US THE SAME."

56 THIRST

Let's talk about the thirst.

The thirst can be for money, attention, knowledge, respect, validation, or whatever. Often the things we want are similar to climbing mountains that don't have peaks. How do we determine how much is enough?

How much money is enough money? How much attention is enough? How many Instagram followers is enough? Anything that can be measured also means it can be compared, and sometimes our motivation for wanting more is really because we're comparing ourselves to others.

Can we put a number beside happiness? We want to be happy all the time, but if we were happy all the time, would we even know after a while? Aren't those other emotions in our lives important as well? If we've never felt misery, how would know we recognize joy? Which emotions teach us the most?

The point I want to get at is that these questions can be infinite, and the answers we find won't be very satisfying. If we take this route of continually just trying to accumulate more things, we may get lost in the process.

The pot of gold at the end of the rainbow, the heaven after we die, and living 'happily ever after' are all simple to understand, but don't make that much sense to how we feel right now. Instead of being lost in the clouds hoping for things to be better, let's worry about right now, where we are, and what we need to do to enjoy that moment.

"ANYTHING THAT CAN BE MEASURED ALSO MEANS IT CAN BE COMPARED, AND SOMETIMES OUR MOTIVATION FOR WANTING MORE IS REALLY BECAUSE WE'RE COMPARING OURSELVES TO OTHERS."

57 DOUBLE STANDARDS

It's that anxiety we get when we know the best option isn't going to be a pleasant one. It may be walking away from a relationship, a job, putting down that ninth cookie, or even simply admitting that we were wrong. Doing what's best isn't always what's easy, and that's why often we may make a choice that gives us the least resistance.

It's not simply an idea that if we knew better, we'd do better. This applies to those around us. Many of the people we are judging are in the same situations as us. They're just trying their best to do what they can with the resources they have.

Life can feel scary and overwhelming. Sometimes, to bring ourselves some temporary relief, we may return to our old patterns of behaviour. Some of those patterns may not be for our best interest, but they do make us feel better in the short terms.

I hear so many people talk about others with judgmental phrases like, "That's so wrong, I can't believe they're doing that, they should know better..." Without taking a moment to jump off their pedestal and see the situation from any other angle.

We tend to judge others by their actions, but ourselves by our intentions. It's a double standard and we're better off being aware of it. Some of you reading this are feeling scared, some of you reading this used to feel the fear, and some of you reading this think it's pure bullsh*t.

Regardless, I feel it needs to be out there for those who needed some of their own thoughts to be a bit clearer.

"WE TEND TO JUDGE OTHERS BY THEIR ACTIONS, BUT OURSELVES BY OUR INTENTIONS. IT'S A DOUBLE STANDARD AND WE'RE BETTER OFF BEING AWARE OF IT."

58 AWKWARD ART

Communication is such an awkward art.

Sometimes we don't know what to say, other times we know exactly what we want to express, but are much too afraid to do it.

Sometimes we say exactly what we want, but once the worlds leave our mouths, or our keyboards, they take a life of their own, and almost become foreign to us after people interpret them in their very own unique ways.

That's how the same sentence can inspire some and offend others.

For those we care about, we have to take extra care in how we communicate with them, and how we interpret the ways they communicate with us. Sometimes we get so caught up in feeling misunderstood that we lose sight that we may also be the ones who are misunderstanding what's being told to us.

"SOMETIMES WE GET SO CAUGHT UP IN FEELING MISUNDERSTOOD THAT WE LOSE SIGHT THAT WE MAY ALSO BE THE ONES WHO ARE MISUNDERSTANDING WHAT'S BEING TOLD TO US."

59 TOM HARDY

I didn't know who Tom Hardy was until I saw the third Batman film, and since he was wearing a mask, I thought he was cast in that film him for his muscles. I figured he must be some sort of heartthrob with the ladies. I didn't see him in another film until I watched the epic 'Mad Max' and again, as an action star, he fit very well, and had very little dialogue in the film.

A friend of my mine had to interview him for a radio show and said he was a very nice and down to earth guy. They ran into each other a few days later, and he was surprised to see that Tom remembered him and engaged him in conversation. Any movie star that's nice to my friends is definitely someone worth checking out.

A photographer I worked with recommended I check out the movie 'Locke' after I told him I was only interested in epic films. And it featured Mr. Hardy. Again, I was intrigued.

This was the first time I saw him act and after the first five minutes, he successfully proved that he was A-list material. The film wasn't a big budget production, it was simple, and relied solely on his performance to make it exceptional. He wasn't a hero, there was no action, no muscles, just raw emotions, and brilliant delivery of dialogue.

It got me thinking about what could have motivated him to take on such a role, or why any actor takes on a small indie film, and that of course is passion. Some of us are looking for the path of least resistance, the easy way, the sure bet. While others seek the challenges, the discomfort, and the opportunities to be outside of their element. Those individuals, like Tom Hardy, use these opportunities to take themselves to a new level and realize a higher potential within themselves.

This isn't exclusive to movie stars. My homeboy, who's also my accountant, loves all the challenges that come with having me as a client. Since I work in multiple disciplines, and make money all around the world, he shows excitement in researching how to handle my finances, and how that's better training him for any future clients. I have other friends in the industry who loathe their accountants because the ones they work with complain that everything is too complicated, and actually push most of the hard work back to the people who asked them to look into things in the first place.

Most people run from challenges, while others run towards them. Deciding which direction you run to is the difference between being A-List, or being just like everyone else.

Which way will you run?

"MOST PEOPLE RUN FROM CHALLENGES, WHILE OTHERS RUN TOWARDS THEM. DECIDING WHICH DIRECTION YOU RUN TO IS THE DIFFERENCE BETWEEN BEING A-LIST, OR BEING JUST LIKE EVERYONE ELSE."

60 WE DECIDE

When sh*t hit the fan for me in my younger years, I would always look to the sky and ask, "Why!?"

I had a victim mentality, I believed life was singling me out and picking on me, I felt that everything that was happening was happening for a reason. So instead of focusing on what was actually happening, I was too busy curled up in a ball feeling sorry for myself.

I was fortunate enough to meet great people along the way that, in not so many words, told me to grow up. They reminded me that the earth would keep turning, and if I wanted things to be or feel better, then I would have to do something about it.

They didn't have to take the time to do so, and I definitely didn't take their words to value the first time I heard it. It took some growing up, and a few more bumps and bruises before the idea successfully sunk in.

One of the biggest gifts we can give ourselves is the responsibility for our happiness.

Life isn't happening to us, we're a part of it. We are a part of this experience of the universe, and right now our energy is concentrated in the form of a walking, talking, breathing, emotionally alive human being. That won't be the case forever. Though energy cannot be created or destroyed in this universe, it does change form, and eventually we will no longer exist in the way that we do right now.
This is crucial idea to understand when we decide the things that are worth our precious time in life. The time we have is very limited and valuable, so let's decide who and what to spend it on, and blame no one else if we waste it.

If we want a greater life, we have to do greater things, it's a very simple idea to understand, but extremely difficult to execute. Nonetheless, it's worth it, I can promise that.

I'm not here to debate fate or divine intervention, I'm here to remind you that you have little control over the events around you. You do, however, have complete and utter control over your own efforts, and your attitudes towards them.

When we focus on aligning ourselves within, the world around us feels a bit more manageable.

"ONE OF THE BIGGEST GIFTS WE CAN GIVE OURSELVES IS THE RESPONSIBILITY FOR OUR HAPPINESS."

61 NO EXPLANATIONS NECESSARY

I get a lot of criticism online. It comes with the territory of being a public figure, mixed with social media giving everyone a platform to voice their unrequested opinions. Almost all of it slides off the skin, but every once and a while someone may say something that penetrates. It doesn't cut through because it's true, but more so that the person has decided to take it upon themselves to tell me WHY I do what I do, or WHY I said what I said, and it's always wrong.

I once had a girl walk up to me in a nightclub asking my why I make songs declaring my love for white girls? I don't have any song about the topic, and I told her that. She told me I was lying, so I asked her to name the song, to which she replied, "You know which one I'm talking about." This is the point where I realized that I wasted moments of my life dignifying such a pointless interaction.

It's very easy to succumb to the urge to defend ourselves in the face of criticism. The reality is that the criticism is validated only once we decide it's worth defending against. As a public figure it's very difficult for me to communicate to a large audience without things being misunderstood, misconstrued, or plain out disagreed with. I learned eventually to stop trying to appease everyone, because that will never happen.

We're better off resisting the urge to defend and justify ourselves to others. The people in our lives that matter most shouldn't require one, and if they do, maybe we need to reevaluate their importance to us.

We can't make progress and excuses at the same time. Much of the time and energy we spend justifying or explaining ourselves to others can be better spent focusing on moving forward. Simply feeling the need to justify our actions is just one additional burden to the decision making process. The fact that not everyone we encounter requires an explanation is a reason in itself.

The older we get, the more we realize how much of a waste of time it actually is trying to make others happy with us. They have their own lives to worry about, and we have ours. If the people around us aren't happy with who we are, we need to change the people, not ourselves. Life is too short for it to work any other way.

"WE'RE BETTER OFF RESISTING THE URGE TO DEFEND AND JUSTIFY OURSELVES TO OTHERS. THE PEOPLE IN OUR LIVES THAT MATTER MOST SHOULDN'T REQUIRE ONE, AND IF THEY DO, MAY BE WE NEED TO REEVALUATE THEIR IMPORTANCE TO US."

62 CHRISTMAS: LILLY'S REVENGE

I'm used to teasing and joking with my friends. We throw little darts and daggers at each other, and nobody takes it personally, it's all about the wittiness. None of the teases are malicious, and everyone knows that their only options are to either laugh along, or shoot back.

One of my favourite targets is Lilly, aka iiSuperWomanii, she has a vibrant positivity, that makes you want to see how far you can go poking her until she pokes back. Every year around the holiday time, Lilly does twelve collaborations for Christmas, where she makes a series of videos with different friends and celebrities.

Every year, this becomes a bigger undertaking, and now it results in her not only writing 12 funny sketches, but also travelling around the world to film them. Her commitment to her fans and her craft is unmatched in my eyes.

One day in December, I was teasing her, as I always do, and noticed her comebacks were much sharper and wittier than normal. She was quick to reply, and those darts and daggers she threw back were not only on point, but also very entertaining.

I realized this had to do with the amount of writing she was doing to squeeze in these twelve important collaborations. It was almost as if all the extra writing had strengthened her funny muscles, and made her a more formidable opponent.

Does this mean I'll stop taking little cheap shots at her? No, you can follow us on twitter to see our public banter never ends. But it does say a lot about the importance of working and sharpening our craft, and how that will benefit us in other aspects of our life.

Whether you're a comedy writer, or practicing a martial art, or painting pictures of flowers, daily repetition of your art is what is going to mold you into the person you want to be. Whether the muscles are creative or physical, the more we train them the better we get, not only in that discipline, but in other ways as well.

Devoting just an hour a day to your craft is enough to make you an expert in your field in five years.

So what are you waiting for, get to work!

"WHETHER THE MUSCLES ARE CREATIVE OR PHYSICAL, THE MORE WE TRAIN THEM THE BETTER WE GET, NOT ONLY IN THAT DISCIPLINE, BUT IN OTHER WAYS AS WELL."

63 SUGAR SHANE

My friend Sugar Shane is one of a kind, a silly genius in every sense of the word. I met him back in 2009 through a mutual friend, and somehow we became very close, very quick. Shane lives in Northern California, but also spent a few years living in LA, so if you find yourself anywhere in the states, and you let him know, Shane will take the 5 hour journey to come see you.

We nicknamed him 'U Turn' because while he would drive, he would get so lost in his stories, that he would always miss his turns, and having to turn around to get us back on track.

While a lot of people will minimize their accomplishments, or allow a good day to be thrown off course by the slightest issue, Shane is the complete opposite. Every new experience leaves him both in awe and superiorly grateful. You can have the same experiences as Shane, and by the end, he'll be able to show you ten things you overlooked throughout that day that were worth appreciating more.

He says 'thank you' a lot, and no matter what you're concerned with, his reply will be, "No no, don't worry I gotcha, we'll figure it out." Sometimes I feel like he fell down, bumped his head, and turned into an eternal optimist.

Shane always finds one thing worth appreciating in any situation, and he authentically means it. He's the epitome of the idea that, 'Life isn't what happens to you, it's how you deal with it.'

Shane is a reminder that we can take control of our day by finding the smiles within it. His generosity teaches me that focusing on giving and helping to those that matter is far more rewarding and fulfilling than isolating ourselves. These aren't traits he was born with. These are the traits he was left with after deciding that some of his decisions in the past weren't helping him in life.

What will it take for the rest of us to see and feel like Shane? Life is amazing, and we know it, but we sometimes allow ourselves to be distracted by everything else, that it passes us by. Even though he misses a few turns every time he hops in the car, he never misses an opportunity to celebrate something small, or to try to put a smile on anyone else's face

Thank you, Sugar Shane.

"...WE CAN TAKE CONTROL OF OUR DAY BY FINDING THE SMILES WITHIN IT."

64 GOOD RIDDANCE

When you're losing someone, the gut instinct is to do, or say, or be anything you can to get them back in your life. It's such a gut wrenching pain when someone exits from your life. I've been there, and the compromises I've made betrayed everything I was, and it was all just to save me some temporary pain.

It may not always feel obvious at the time (who am I kidding, it'll NEVER feel obvious at the time), but as things play out, we can realize that some of the people that leave our lives, take with them a lot of bullsh*t too.

This frees us up to breathe a bit, and though it will feel uncomfortable when we first lose them, it's up to us to find (or create) the silver lining from any situation.

We're all going to experience loss in our lives, and though we didn't sign up for it (or see it coming), we'll be better off for being prepared regardless.

I've loved and lost, and I've loved and left, and I'm sure some of those lovely individuals from my past are glad to see me gone. This life is what we make it, and crawling up into a ball after getting dumped isn't going make it much.

Focusing on what we have, and not what we've lost is a great first step to regaining our balance on this journey.

"I'VE LOVED I'VE LOVED

AND LOST, AND LEFT…"

65 WHAT CAN GO RIGHT?

It took so long for me to put my work out into the public (including this book) because I always worry about what could go wrong. Having a negative attitude, combined with a vivid imagination is very counter-productive. Only when I gained some excitement towards all the great things can happen once my work is out, did the work start bringing itself to life.

Let's shift the focus from what can go wrong to what can go right.

We so often talk ourselves out of attempting amazing things because we're afraid, and that's normal. Though it's a bit odd that the same brain that came up with the idea to go to the gym almost instantly begins giving us reasons to stay home, that oddity exists in all of us, and we're better off being aware of its existence.

One of the best solutions to combat these thoughts is to simply get moving. We only have a few seconds from thinking up our great idea to changing our mind, and in that window of time we need to get off our butts and make something happen, even of it's just a small step.

We may get overwhelmed and think off all the reasons why we can fail, and if you look around, that's why we're a culture of shattered and deferred dreams.

Be the exception to that rule. Get moving.

" WE ONLY HAVE A FEW SECONDS FROM THINKING UP OUR GREAT IDEA TO CHANGING OUR MIND, AND IN THAT WINDOW OF TIME WE NEED TO GET OFF OUR BUTTS AND MAKE SOMETHING HAPPEN, EVEN OF IT'S JUST A SMALL STEP."

66 ALIGNMENT

Sometimes we find it easier to compartmentalize our lives. We can act as if everything we do doesn't directly affect other aspects of our lives, but they totally do. We're complicated creatures that are composed of multiple dimensions of elements that all require maintenance. That includes your mind, body, soul, spirit, attitude, or whatever else you attribute to your being. It's easy in this life to lose track of everything, and not realize how interconnected all these elements really are.

I know when I was struggling to revisit the gym regularly, it was a friend that said "Go to the gym simply because it feels good to go, don't worry about it for any other reason." That worked for me, and all the other benefits of going to the gym automatically came along with it. As animals, we can't function unless our basic needs are met. As humans, we've developed new 'needs' and we don't feel optimal until they're achieved.

We're far better off focusing on identifying our unique needs and fulfilling them so we can achieve some sort of balance in life. I can't sit and write a chapter of this book if I'm hungry, nor can I work well if I'm dealing with heartbreak, or stressed out about my finances. Life will never be so easy that we'll be able to put it into cruise control, and ride off into the sunset. There will always be obstacles, bumps, potholes and curves on the road, but having ourselves in alignment will best prepare us to deal with those.

"Just as your car runs more smoothly and requires less energy to go faster and farther when the wheels are in perfect alignment, you'll perform better when your thoughts, feelings, emotions, goals, and values are in balance."   --Brian Tracy

"THERE WILL ALWAYS BE OBSTACLES, BUMPS, POTHOLES AND CURVES ON THE ROAD, BUT HAVING OURSELVES IN ALIGNMENT WILL BEST PREPARE US TO DEAL WITH THOSE."

67 CO-EXIST

Don't let anyone hold your feelings hostage.

Our emotions belong to us, and although we should spend energy daily learning how to understand and work with them, it's not in our best interest to cater them to the whims of others.

I grew up in a social circle where my friends were always teasing each other. That prepared me to be quick on my toes, and also thickened my skin (which has come in handy quite a bit since I got a lil popular). There are often instances where I'm around people who react to things dramatically different than myself, and that's okay, we can learn from each other, but neither of us is obligated to feel what the others feel.

If events around the world pull on your heart strings, that's great. If it's all the same noise to you, that's fine as well. There's always a bit of emotional blackmail going on when people want to rally us towards their causes. Before we get sucked into any kind of hype we should remember that we're allowed to feel the way we do, whether that agrees with anyone else or not.

The ability to co-exist with people who think, look, feel, and act differently is a talent, and an indicator that you are an open-minded, evolved human being. There are many people who refuse this level of openness, because the idea of things different to them is different. Just wave and smile at them as you keep it moving.

Feel what you feel, learn from what you feel, and if you have good, share what you feel. Whether it's with your friends, your art, or even the punching bag. Every emotion we have is a gift.

"THE ABILITY TO CO-EXIST WITH PEOPLE WHO THINK, LOOK, FEEL, AND ACT DIFFERENTLY IS A TALENT, AND AN INDICATOR THAT YOU ARE AN OPEN-MINDED, EVOLVED HUMAN BEING."

68 NAKED

It was clear that a year after leaving my job to chase my dreams, I had only dug myself into a deeper hole. I had maxed out my credit cards and line of credit. My supposed partner in crime and business partner jumped ship after I was of no more use to him, and all I had left was a mountain of debt, and thick cloak of embarrassment.

I was naked.

I didn't want to leave the apartment, I was still hoping that everything was a misunderstanding, that the business deals that had been taking so long to "process" would arrive with a giant juicy cheque to erase all of this stress in one clean swoop. But the waiting was torturous.

So I took Nyquil to sleep, hoping that when I wake up, everything would have worked itself out. I took a lot of Nyquil.

Every time I woke up, there were no updates, there was no hope, no magical cheques had arrived in the mail, only more bills, and more worries.

My family wanted me to come over. I didn't want to go.
My friends wanted to hang out, I didn't want to.
I was too busy feeling sorry for myself.

When we're at low points in life, we feel naked, and that makes us want to further isolate ourselves from the world. We don't want anyone to see us, because we're ashamed of what they're going to see, or at least what we think they'll see.

I sat in a lawn chair in my empty apartment, watching cartoons and eating breakfast, and then the rest of the day would be spent taking very long walks, hoping to find clarity, or a miracle. The miracles never came; neither did the clarity. Instead, a memory sparked.

It was a conversation I had with a friend of a friend in Delhi a month before. He said, "Being naked in front of everyone is either the most terrifying or liberating experience you can have, you have to decide."

No one was coming to save me, no one was obligated to do so. The only reason I was having an problems was because I was devoting so much energy to pretending that everything was fine.Everything wasn't fine, and first I had to admit that to myself, and not be afraid to admit that to anyone else.

It really is liberating when you let it all hang out, when you don't have to keep track of your lies, and who you tell them to. The people who find pleasure in your failures always will, so who cares if they know you're not doing well. The people that love you, will love you regardless, and if they change up because they find out something new about you, well good riddance to them.

Not only was I naked, I was covered in guilt, shame, embarrassment, disappointment and unhappiness. I had to wash those off to even recognize myself. Every time I scrub a layer off, I find something new beneath, I continue to scratch away the surface of this dirty to what appears. I know this is going to be a life long journey.

It took another three years to get myself back to zero. Paying off debt is not as challenging as avoiding sinking into resentment and regret for all my past mistakes. The more I shed and let go, the more of my naked self revealed. I had scares and wounds I didn't realize existed, and it was important to address them for them to heal.

"How much has to be explored and discarded before reaching the naked flesh of feeling." -Claude Debussy

We all have layers of pain on our naked bodies, and we have to scratch and scrub to see what's beneath the surface. Let's make the decision to allow this nakedness to liberate us, rather than confine us to more pain and loneliness.

I was naked, and I still am, and I'm proud that I can be.

"EVERYTHING WASN'T FINE, AND FIRST I HAD TO ADMIT THAT TO MYSELF, AND NOT BE AFRAID TO ADMIT THAT TO ANYONE ELSE. "

69 PRISON BREAK

We can easily become the prisoners of our own thoughts.

Even if we know what we want, or where we need to be, we often end up building our own barriers that prevent us from getting there. Those barriers are commonly motivated by the fears we cook up in our imaginations.

Recently someone approached me with a question I get very often. He asked, "How did you deal with all the criticisms of putting your work out there? I could never be able to deal with that!" This question revealed the ideas he had already formed in his head, and it expressed the excuses he made for not pursuing the life he truly wanted.

To break out of the bars we construct in our minds, we have to flip the switch and convert our thoughts into actions. Doing is always better than thinking, and over-thinking will only cause under-doing.

The first step in gaining some freedom from the prisons we construct for ourselves is to acknowledge that we're constructing these prisons in the first place. Don't finger-point, place blame. You should always start with yourself, your own personal power, and your responsibility to have the life you want to live.

I'm not going to say it's all in your head, but you know, a lot of it is. Taking steps gain freedom from those self-imposed prisons will also free you from the BS that holds you down in the outside world.

"THE FIRST STEP IN GAINING SOME FREEDOM FROM THE PRISONS WE CONSTRUCT FOR OURSELVES IS TO ACKNOWLEDGE THAT WE'RE CONSTRUCTING THESE PRISONS IN THE FIRST PLACE."

70 THE INVISIBLE AUDIENCE

Who's acceptance do we require before we feel like we've made it? Is it our parents? The Academy? Our peers? What voices of judgment we are hearing in our heads? Who are we trying to prove wrong?

The wealthiest people I know work the hardest, and show off the least. It's all the wanna-be-fancy-folk that spend the extra money to look like they're in a higher tax bracket, and try to be in all the "right" places. What they eventually realize is they're only catering to people like themselves - people who are desperate to prove something to somebody.

But who's the somebody we're trying to impress?

I used to be teased as a child for the way I look. I had a crooked nose and buck teeth, but that ball of hair on top of my head is what defined me, and that was all the other kids would see. Then the beard started growing in awkwardly, and things felt even worse. Fast forward a few years, and I have people in the fashion industry go into detail describing how beautiful my bone structure is, and how handsome I am. But you know what? That's not enough. I've even been paid great sums of money to model, and that wasn't enough either. Even though I thought I wanted their approval, receiving it did very little for the way I felt about myself.

It was then that I realized, the real person that was thinking low of me... was me.

I don't know now where the kids are that teased me, and even if I did, it wouldn't make much differences rubbing my success in their face. The fact will always remain that the most important opinion that matters is the one that we have of ourselves.

Sure our parents, friends, family, media and society can play a huge part in shaping those views, but those views are still internal. Very little validation, acceptance, and accolades from the outside world can change what we've set ourselves up to believe.

I think what's necessary to feel better about ourselves is a different journey for each of us, but the first step is realizing who we really need to impress.

Self-love is a skill, start practicing.

"...THE MOST IMPORTANT OPINION THAT MATTERS IS THE ONE THAT WE HAVE OF OURSELVES."

71 MONKEY ON MY BACK

I was always afraid to speak out and ask questions. Sometimes that fear was because I was scared that people wouldn't like me if I did, other times it was because I afraid of hearing an response I wouldn't like. I would always imagine such a tragic and apocalyptic worse case scenarios, and that fear would keep me from making any progress. I noticed other people doing things I was too afraid of and trying to figure out how.

The things we feel and give to ourselves are the doors we allow the rest of the world to access. If we don't have love for ourselves, then that door is closed for others to love us as well. If we talk ourselves out of doing what we think is best, then we're inviting the worse into our lives. No one can stand up for us or our happiness if we don't do it for ourselves.

I was afraid, and I still am, but every so often, I muster up enough energy to move with the fear hanging on my back. More times than not, the outcomes are magical. Most of my worst fears exist only in my head, and even if things don't go my way, it's never as bad as what I imagined it might be. The mantra I have to remind myself of is "if you don't do it for yourself, who will?"

Gone are the days of our childhood when we can rely on someone else to take care of us and sort everything out. The older we get, the more responsibility we hold for our own well being, and although that responsibility can feel overwhelming, it's the reality of all of our situations.

I mention earlier in the book that fear can be a compass or a roadblock; it's up to us to decide. How much we value ourselves decides what we're willing to push through to have the life we want. I hope my fears guide me to where I need to go, I refuse to let it weigh me down anymore.

"I WAS AFRAID, AND I STILL AM, BUT EVERY SO OFTEN, I MUSTER UP ENOUGH ENERGY TO MOVE WITH THE FEAR HANGING ON MY BACK."

72 LAW & ORDER

It was 2009 and I was trying to watch Law & Order in the kitchen, and in comes my father and his father, my Papa Ji. They proceed to have a conversation right in front of the television, completely oblivious to the fact that I'm trying to watch it. After a few loud coughs, and other obvious signals, it's clear that they either won't be getting the hint, or don't care to. Frustrated, I get up and head to my room to go pack for my trip. I was flying out to Thailand for a three-week adventure early the following morning.

Papa Ji was still in bed when I was getting ready to leave, and I didn't want to wake him. My folks dropped me off at the airport, and my adventure was beginning.

I could write half a book about my adventures in Thailand, the people I met, and the sights I saw, but what only mattered was the email I received half way through the trip.

It was from my sister, and simply read "call home when you can"

Most of the time when someone asks you to call them, you think it's something bad, but it turns out to be something silly and your worries melt as you realize how ridiculous you were for getting so worked up in first place.

This wasn't one of those times.

I call home from the hotel room, and my sister picks up.

"Papa Ji passed away"

It's odd that I can remember exactly where I was, and what corner of the room

I was sitting, when I heard the news; right up to how the tears began to blur my vision.

A few days after I left, my grandfather had a stroke, and began to recover, but things took a turn for the worse, and he began to have swelling in his brain, and eventually fell into a coma that he wasn't waking up from. He was taken off life support shortly after, and my family felt it best not to tell me about any of this while I was away.

With hands shaking and tears in my eyes, I struggled to get words out. Half of me was trying to figure out what I needed to do to come home, while the other half was trying to process what was happening.

My dad got on the phone:

"Dad, what happened?"

"I'm coming home, I don't know how long it'll take but.."

"Uhh, I need to come for the funeral..."

"He's gone"

"Why? Everyone else in the family was around his bed when he died, and they couldn't save him, what are you going to do?"

"No, you don't, you need to enjoy the rest of your trip. There's no point coming home. Make the most of the life you have, that's the best choice right now"

At this point my entire face was leaking. My sister took the phone and supported my dad's decision to encourage me to stay, she said there wouldn't be any point in making such a long trip home.

I didn't get to say goodbye, I don't even remember my last words to him, all I remember is kissing my teeth as he stood in front to the television talking to my dad. I don't remember the last time hugged him, or even what our last conversation was about.

What a horrible person I was.

For the remainder of the trip, the more fun I had, the more I remembered that my father was sitting at home mourning his own. I would cry in the bathroom before and after every outing. I would try my hardest to remember my grandfather's last words to me. I would wonder if I was home, would I have discovered him earlier, and possibly saved his life. We all have these types of thoughts, and they're both pointless and painful.

Five years later, I still don't remember my last conversation with my Papa Ji.

My father had lost both his parents in a span of a year, and though it's an inevitable reality, it's something we make a lot of effort to avoid remembering.

Those experiences changed him, I can't say whether it was for the best or worse, but that phone call wasn't the last time he told me to "Have fun, do what you want, you'll be dead soon".

A year later that was his reply when I told him I wanted to quit my job as a teacher to try this Humble The Poet thing out full time.

We've all suffered loss, and most of that loss wasn't expected, the loss of my Papa Ji forced my father to re-evaluate his priorities in his own life. He spent less time worrying about household, and more time about the people in it. He was a grandfather first now, and would prefer waddling along behind my nieces and nephews than discussing important issues within the family.

I guess it's up to us to decide whether the losses we experiences will become tragedies or blessings.

My Papa Ji was walking and talking, and showed no signs of slowing down a week before his stroke. It's a reminder that anything can happen at any time. For some people that's a depressing reminder, for myself, that's fuel for me to make the most of however much time I have left.

I remember being 8 years old, and winning a foot race at a local community tournament, I got a trophy and everything. The next day I had a foot race with my Papa Ji at the park, and he creamed me. I was in utter shock that his old guy could beat me, I had a trophy after all.

Maybe that's the only memory I need from him, the first time I was humbled.

"...IT'S UP TO US TO DECIDE WHETHER THE LOSSES WE EXPERIENCES WILL BECOME TRAGEDIES OR BLESSINGS."

73 MISTAKES

Don't avoid mistakes, and don't regret mistakes. Our mistakes are a part of the process, and we should look forward to making many of them throughout our lives. We sabotage ourselves when we're overly cautious about things. We imagine potential consequences and those thoughts trigger fears, and those fears slam on the breaks. Once the breaks are locked in, we're not making any progress at all. We're simply existing huddled in a proverbial corner of life.

Mistakes have a lot of value in them, but only if we take the time to dig around for the lessons. There are no failures, only jewels of wisdom to be extracting when things don't go our way. The enemy isn't the mistake at all, but rather the fear of making them. The most successful people in the world aren't afraid to get their hands dirty, be uncomfortable or make mistakes. Be like the most successful people in the world.

Many of our past regrets are associated with mistakes, big and small. That is simply because we found no benefit in those events occurring. None of us have a crystal ball. We don't know the consequences of our actions and when things don't turn out the way we hoped, we can either mope about it, or start paying attention to see where what wisdom and experience is being gifted our way. While we're allowing these lessons to reveal themselves, it's essential that we remember to keep moving.

Let's reevaluate our relationship with our mistakes. Nothing is our friend, and nothing is our enemy. Everything, including our mistakes, is our teacher.

"NOTHING IS OUR FRIEND, AND NOTHING IS OUR ENEMY. EVERYTHING, INCLUDING OUR MISTAKES, IS OUR TEACHER."

74 QUESTIONS ARE BETTER THAN ANSWERS

Admitting that we know nothing, makes room for us to learn anything.

A closed mind can't be taught anything, and that's the danger of thinking we have all of the answers. I don't like to look at life as a problem to be solved, but rather an experience to be had. It's much more exciting that way.

Life can be frustrating, and that will naturally make us want to seek guidance from others. The reality with that however, is that people may have great experiences and wisdom to share, but they're still in the same boat as the rest of us.

The questions will always be more important than the answers. Never blindly follow those before you, but rather seek what they're seeking.

It's a scary thought to have, and it's why we turn to those before us for guidance and wisdom, because after all, they seem to be doing alright. Those feelings are normal, but just remember to allow the information to flow in you, and be willing to let go what doesn't agree with your being.

You have more wisdom inside you than I could ever sell ya.

Never stop learning.

"THE QUESTIONS WILL ALWAYS BE MORE IMPORTANT THAN THE ANSWERS. NEVER BLINDLY FOLLOW THOSE BEFORE YOU, BUT RATHER SEEK WHAT THEY'RE SEEKING."

75 FIRST KISS

We can't always control the outcome, and that's totally scary. Even though some of our most painful moments were also the moments we learned from the most, we really don't want any more painful moments and that's normal.

Just like a first kiss, it's not the end game that ends up having the most impact, it's the anticipation. In this case, the anticipation feeds a lot of fear, and fear can paralyze us, making it even more difficult to move forward.

I'm not writing this because these are things I've experienced and overcome. I'm writing this because these are things I've experienced and continue to experience. The difference now is that I respect the importance of these experiences, and make a painfully large effort to work within them to grow.

The fear does not go away, if anything it may get even more intense. Sometimes the greatest fears I feel are when good things are happening in life, whether that's fear of losing what I have, or fear that my present is the highlight of my life, and everything will go downhill from here (aren't we such great fear-making machines).

It's a pointless battle to fight the fears we have, so let's instead work to understand, and move despite them. Bravery doesn't exist in the absence of fear, it exists in the face of it.

Understanding what we're afraid of, and why are the firsts steps to having a better relationship with those fears, so they don't get in the way.

"BRAVERY DOESN'T EXIST IN THE ABSENCE OF FEAR, IT EXISTS IN THE FACE OF IT."

76 IS IT WORTH IT?

We have to take responsibility for the people we allow into our lives.
This, like everything else in life, is easier said than done. Some of the people in our lives that cause us unwanted grief may be in the bedroom next door, and it may feel like confronting the grief is unavoidable.

The key word is "feel."

We will be better off when we love ourselves enough to stand up for ourselves and how we deserve to be treated. And you know, that may require us to get a bit uncomfortable.

The only question you have to ask yourself after that is, "Is it worth it?"

I can't answer that question for anyone else but myself. Lauryn Hill taught me years ago, writing, "If everything must go, then go, that's how I choose to live." We won't get the life we wish for, we can only get the life we work for. Sometimes that life isn't about gaining things that we want, sometimes it's more about letting things (and people) go.

Letting go doesn't mean we have to run away from home, it means we have to actively no longer allow people who do not deserve space in our hearts, to have the ability to affect us. That's a slow process, but we have to start somewhere.

Not everyone can be avoided, but we can limit the calories we throw their way. Respect the limited amount of energy you have, and only spend it on those you feel deserve it.

> "WE WON'T GET THE LIFE
> WE WISH FOR,
> WE CAN ONLY GET
> THE LIFE WE WORK FOR."

77
SAND IN YOUR HOURGLASS

Once time is spent, it can't be made back. My mother would tell me stories during late nights in the car, after trips to the Gurudwara. She would translate the stories told during the evening procession, and stress to me that I had to spend my time wisely because once it's gone, I don't get it back.

I was ten at the time, and the concept of forever or even the next five years was foreign. A couple decades later, long term thinking still eludes me, but I'm realizing now how valuable the time I have now really is. Maybe the older we get, we value it a bit more because we know it's running out.

I don't know when I'll take my last breath, neither does any one who's reading this. Some of us act as if it won't be happening any time soon, but who really knows? All we know for sure is that the present moment is the only time we have.

My mother would also say, "Don't find the time, make the time," And though she was likely making reference to things like cleaning my room, or other situations where I complained about not having time, the point remains the same.

If you think you don't have time to do something, you're lying to yourself. The reality is you're not making the time to do it, and need to ask yourself why that is. Every grain of sand in our hourglass is a priceless jewel, and how we spend those jewels is a reflection of our priorities, and the life we want.

Are you spending your time the way you want?

"EVERY GRAIN OF SAND IN OUR HOURGLASS IS A PRICELESS JEWEL, AND HOW WE SPEND THOSE JEWELS IS A REFLECTION OF OUR PRIORITIES, AND THE LIFE WE WANT."

78 LEAN ON ME?

If we don't lean on others, then no one can let us down

I know that's the beauty of relationships, but really it's the double edged sword. Dependencies form expectations, and with expectations can come big disappointments. This isn't a romantic thought, but I'm not here to here to sell romance. I'm not here to sell anything, I am here to remind you of something you already know.

Our emotions and feelings exist inside, so why do we look to the outside world to have a lasting effect on them? Our thoughts, mindset, and focus are what will determine our emotions and how we feel about our lives. When we focus inward, we can create almost everything we need to feel great about life, and that can even result in a little extra that we can share with the world.

When we continually lean on others, we may never develop the strength to stand on our own. If we can't stand on our own, then we can't support anyone else who may need us during a rough patch. It's the same with love, attention, affection and validation. If we're constantly thirsting for it on the outside, we may never learn how to discover it within. That does a disservice to not only us, but also the people in our lives when we can't learn emotional independence.

Life will always feel better when we're able to give more than we take, and for that to happen, we need to focus on our own foundation, and focus on finding all the wonderful things that reside within us.

Then we'll be in a position to not only stand strong, but also to help others do the same.

"WHEN WE CONTINUALLY LEAN ON OTHERS, WE MAY NEVER DEVELOP THE STRENGTH TO STAND ON OUR OWN."

79 THE CREATIVE BONE IS CONNECTED TO THE...

"An essential aspect of creativity is not being afraid to fail." - Edwin Land

It's essential that we create, whether individually or as a collective. I remember watching something on television talking about the stresses that can come to people that don't have a creative outlet.

Creativity isn't exclusive to music, writing, dancing et cetera. Everyday people are creating and raising children. The acts of bringing something to life and watching it evolve is a gift that we have as a species, and we have so many options to make it happen.

I wrote a book, and it blows my mind that the book may be read by folks long after I'm gone. I have creative projects on the internet that will also outlive me. I've always seen my creative projects as my children, they're definitely not as fun to create, but they do grow and take on ilves of their own.

We all have some kind of creative bone in us, and we'll enjoy it most when we're creating simply for the sake of creating, and not for the approval of an audience or any other type of validation. There's no failure in creativity when the journey is all the matters.

What do you want to create?

> "THERE'S NO FAILURE IN CREATIVITY WHEN THE JOURNEY IS ALL THE MATTERS."

80 SOMETIMES WE'RE THE BAD GUYS

We can often spend so much time looking at the world, seeing what's wrong with it, seeing how it impacts us, that we may turn a blind eye to the impact we have on others.

We reminisce on our heartbreaks, but what about when we're the heartbreakers, the cheaters, the people that were selfish? It's an interesting exercise considering how prevalent it's become to feel like a victim of life.

Eating beef contributes to more world pollution than driving a car (because of the methane). Drinking milk supports veal (yes, you ethical vegetarians, do a little research). Many of the cell phones we've used weren't built under ideal labour conditions as well.

We are all, in one way shape or form, part of the problem.

This chapter isn't here to make you feel bad, if anything, to do the opposite. We're all the problems and we can all be the solution. Very few of us are mere victims. We're contributors to this complex system of life, and not all part of that system are romantic and wonderful. Many of these systems are designed to crumble the moment someone tries to make them fair.

It's reality, and developing a healthy relationship with it should be a priority.

So next time you find that you're about to feel sorry for yourself, just don't.

"WE ARE ALL,
IN ONE WAY SHAPE OR FORM,
PART OF THE PROBLEM."

81 REBEL WITH A CAUSE

Living up to other people's expectations are exhausting... And that energy can be spent doing better things. It's totally normal to have relationships that have expectations, our parents expect something of us, so does society, so do our friends, and the people we work with. But if we spend too much time focusing on what they want, we take away from time that can be spent discovering who we are.

Anyone who thinks they know themselves completely, is living a lie. Self discovery is an ongoing process, and the longer we explore, the deeper we'll go. We'll only stop learning and growing when we're dead. Much of how we identify ourselves before discovery is based on the expectations and norms of those around us.

"Everyone else is walking a certain path, maybe I should walk that path."You may say that to yourself sometimes, and that's a normal thought to have. It sure beats having to figure things out for yourself and reinventing the wheel, but eventually that beaten path may lose it's appeal. And that'll happen pretty fast if you feel pressured to walk it.

People think instantly this means to be rebellious towards the people we love, but that's not really the case. It means take the time to actually discover what we really want in life, and then have the courage to share that with people trying to push us in another direction.

Life is too short to live it solely to please other people. We're all unique creatures. The more we tap into that, the more amazing things we end up sharing with the world.

"SELF DISCOVERY IS AN

THE LONGER WE
WE'LL GO."

ONGOING PROCESS...

EXPLORE, THE DEEPER

82 PILLARS

"The most important relationship you have is with yourself." – Diane Von Furstenberg"

Everything we feel we're lacking we can easily begin seeking outside of ourselves. Often, that includes love. We seek love from others. Acceptance, validation, comfort, security, confidence are all part of the list. Though it feels great, and it's really a human thing to do, it can lead to some unpleasant circumstances when feelings change.

Kahlil Gibran (and if you don't know who that is, shame on you and start Googling) describes lovers as pillars that require distance from each other to hold up a temple. Even in a relationship, both parties need to have their own ability to hold things up. This means not building relationships on dependence. We're better off standing up straight, and not leaning one way or the other.

When we look within for many of the things we feel we need, we'll tap into an unlimited source of love, energy, creativity, and imagination that not only can feed us, but can also be shared with others. The need to share and help will yield better relationships than the need to receive.

It's easier said than done, and I experience the same feelings of loneliness that everyone else feels, it's a matter of respecting the feelings and allowing them to happen, but not letting them govern the type of relationships we foster.

Love yourself first. After that, you can share what you have left with those you care about.

"WHEN WE LOOK WITHIN FOR MANY OF THE THINGS WE FEEL WE NEED, WE'LL TAP INTO AN UNLIMITED SOURCE OF LOVE, ENERGY, CREATIVITY, AND IMAGINATION THAT NOT ONLY CAN FEED US, BUT CAN ALSO BE SHARED WITH OTHERS."

83 SIKH KNOWLEDGE

One evening I receive an email from Kanwar, aka Anit, aka Sikh Knowledge. The emailed contained a list of personal passwords and information with the heading "just in case."

I wasn't the only friend on the email, and although the email was a surprise, we all knew what he meant by "just in case"

The death threats had intensified. People wanted to end his life, because he's gay.

We all jokingly replied, arguing over who was going to get that ugly lamp in his apartment, and who got dibs over his record collection. We use humour to mask some of the other intense emotions we have, sometimes it's the only way to cope.

People find it offensive that Kanwar exists; they find it offensive that he's gay; they find it offensive that he uses the name Sikh Knowledge as an artist. Some are so offended that they took it upon themselves to threaten his life.

Without Sikh Knowledge, there would be no Humble The Poet. Our work together is what put me on the map, and his support is the main reason I continue to move forward. It's both scary and frustrating when you feel a loved one is in danger, and there's nothing you can do.

I realize that there's very little that can be done towards people who hold strong beliefs of intolerance. It comes from a place of fear and discomfort with them, and it's difficult to address something won't admit exists.

But things aren't hopeless.

There's a newer generation, and they're empty vessels, which have yet to be taught to hate, because hate needs to be taught. This new generation has the opportunity to look past superficial things like skin colour, or whom a person chooses to love, and instead has a chance to judge a person based on who they are.

These death threats from cowards an ocean away are troubling, but Kanwar hasn't lost a step. His struggles have made him a wonderful, wise, and strong person. He doesn't focus on trying to undo a past, but instead, his energy is focused on building a better future, where people don't have to live in a world of "just in case."

"...HATE NEEDS TO BE TAUGHT."

84 HOLD LESS, BALANCE MORE

Balance isn't a one-time thing.

We don't simply achieve balance in life. We don't have the ability to press pause, or auto-pilot, and it'll be smooth sailing from there on in. We achieve balance for a short period of time, then something (or someone) will come and knock us off course, and that's life.

Sometimes over-thinking, and over-trying in life actually makes things more difficult and confusing. There's a charm to simplicity, so one of the best ways I've found to achieve balance a bit more often, is to be holding onto a lot less sh*t. We'll be better off shedding ourselves of excess baggage of regrets, negative thoughts, and energy draining people. That will free up some room for more important things, as well as make life feel a bit lighter.

The world is going to continue to turn regardless of what we're doing with our lives, so if we want to do our best, we just have to keep turning with it. When sh*t hits the fan, curling up into the fetal position and blaming the universe will do very little to help our cause.

"SOMETIMES OVER-THINKING, AND OVER-TRYING IN LIFE ACTUALLY MAKES THINGS MORE DIFFICULT AND CONFUSING."

85 A LESSON FROM L.A. TRAFFIC

Sometimes it's our lack of patience that leads to our lack of progress.

Things take time. We have to respect that. Things seem impossible before they're done, and easy after the fact. Whatever we want to achieve we have to be mindful of the time it takes to make things happen.

We over-estimate how much we can get done in a day. I'm typing this as I sit in Los Angeles, the place where 90% of your life will be spent in a car to get 10% of the productivity out of your day. But at the same time we underestimate how much we can accomplish in the long run.

When building a wall, we'll get overwhelmed thinking about the grandeur of the task, especially if it's a big one. But if we simply focus on laying one brick at a time, the progress will add up. Anything we want to accomplish in life will be easier to manage if we break it down into tiny pieces and handle them one at a time.

Anything from writing a book, to taking inches off that tummy will take time, focus on the baby steps and let them build up. And you know, a year from now you'll be glad you did.

"ANYTHING WE WANT TO ACCOMPLISH IN LIFE WILL BE EASIER TO MANAGE IF WE BREAK IT DOWN INTO TINY PIECES AND HANDLE THEM ONE AT A TIME."

86 ROLLERCOASTERS

"It must be nice to not have a nine-to-five, work when you want, that freedom must be amazing." If I had a nickel for every time someone said this to me, I wouldn't be a millionaire, but my pockets would most definitely drag as I walked.

I gave up a nine-to-five (well more of a 8:45-3:30, by the time I was at the end of my wits, but who's counting), and I thought I would have this glamorous life of travel, and creativity and adventure. In some ways, I do, but like every other ungrateful and adaptive human being, I've gotten use to a bit of it to the point that I may not notice.

I traded the eight hour days and five day work weeks for a life that is 24/7 work. I may not be productive from wake to sleep, but I can promise you without a doubt that my productivity consumes my mind from wake to sleep. There's a cloud of doubt and anxiety that floats over my head, but that's the life of a creative. It's goodbye to the predictable (and reliable) paycheck that comes every two weeks, and hello to good months, and bad months as well.

Everybody's life is a rollercoaster, and when you chase your dreams, the only thing that changes about that rollercoaster is it gets a lot more intense. The highs are much higher, and the lows go so deep, you aren't sure if you're going to survive. The wins seem to fade very quickly, while the low points seem to linger on.

Experiencing this reality was a challenge for me because I was all like, "Hey wait a minute, I thought chasing my dreams will let me live happily ever after." Obviously it doesn't, and after some time, I became okay with that, because although chasing my dreams isn't giving me everlasting happiness, it is giving me something far more valuable and stimulating.

Chasing your dreams won't make you happy, but if you keep at it, I promise you won't be bored very often. The rollercoaster only gets more intense and scary, and really, that's the reason we ride them in the first place.

Life is an adventure, and I'm strapped in, making weird faces, trying not to throw up all over myself. Some days are great, while others are not so wonderful, but no two are alike, and I could never imagine doing anything else.

If you decide to jump out on a limb and chase your passions, don't do it with the expectations of a fairy tale ending, because you will be sorely disappointed. Instead, understand you're signing up to turn your life into an adventure story. There will be action, suspense, danger, and pain. Every moment will not be the greatest, but as a whole, it'll make for a wild ride.

"CHASING YOUR DREAMS WON'T MAKE YOU HAPPY, BUT IF YOU KEEP AT IT, I PROMISE YOU WON'T BE BORED VERY OFTEN."

87 "AREN'T YOU HUMBLE THE POET?"

It was late spring 2010, I was helping a community group set up an event that was happening by my house when I got a call that my mother's mother (we called her Chachi) passed away. I was 5 minutes from the hospital and arrived quickly to see my family in the waiting room.

My Chachi was an old, wrinkly, cuddly grandmother who always had a smile on her face. She had grey eyes, but you would have to look deep into them to notice. She had her name tattooed up high on her forearm because, in her words, "to hide it from the police".

She would stare at her reflection in the television and think she was watching a show. She would call our house, and think the answering machine was a white lady talking, a believe she had the wrong number. My Chachi was just the most adorable creation I ever came across.

When I was a child I would sleep in the bed with her, and she would call me "Beeba Puth" (that meant good boy). My grandmother was simply a source of happiness and squishy hugs. I had many conversations with her, most I didn't fully comprehend, but all of them I enjoyed.

She past away in her late 90's and was still lucid, and self-sufficient.

In the hospital, we took turns entering the room where her body lay. My mom and her older sister stayed in the room as we all shuffled in and out to see her one last time. My mother lost her father when she was 13, and if you've been reading this book in order, you'll realize that this was the last of my grandparents. If you still have grandparents in your life, please go give them a hug for the rest of us who can't.

As I stepped out of the little room where her body lay, I began to notice a few of the volunteers working at the hospital were orbiting around us. They were staring, and one approached me nervously asking, "Hey, aren't you Humble The Poet?"

Back in 2010, it was still a big deal for me to get recognized, even if it was at the hospital down the street from my house, but this time it felt weird. I was at the hospital to see my grandmother, who had just passed hours before, but these volunteers didn't know that; I wasn't sure they would even care.

I politely smiled, said yes, and walked towards my grieving family. They must have got the hint, because they didn't follow. There's no training manual on how to be a public figure, and deal with attention at all the wrong times. It's easy to forget that others are human beings, and being human is hard, especially with an audience.

As my name gains more traction, it isn't a struggle to remain normal, normal is what I am. The challenge is dealing with the abnormal treatment I get from others. This journey, just like the one you're on, is all trial and error. We learn as we go, make mistakes a long the way, and pray we learn from them.

I miss my Chachi, I see her face in my mother's. That both comforts and terrifies me at the same time.

"THIS JOURNEY, JUST LIKE THE ONE YOU'RE ON, IS ALL TRIAL AND ERROR. WE LEARN AS WE GO, MAKE MISTAKES A LONG THE WAY, AND PRAY WE LEARN FROM THEM."

88. THE TRUTH WILL NOT SET YOU FREE

If anything, the truth will take the simple black and white view some may have of the world, and turn it upside down and make them uncomfortable. The truth resists simplicity, it resists comfort, but people appreciate simplicity, as well as comfort, so they may not really want the truth anywhere close to them.

The truth definitely won't make you popular, and if anything, it'll scare away some of the people around you. The truth may not agree with what everyone else is doing, and everyone else doesn't want to hear that.

There's no need for the truth when there's someone out there always telling you what you already agree with. We feel special when we're validated, and we enjoy hearing the things we like to hear. It's why politicians can break promises and still get re-elected.

The truth is also a personal thing, though people often mistake their opinions for facts, our wiring and life experiences help shape our understanding of the world unique to only us. The truth for one may not apply to another, that's difficult to grasp or accept, but that's part of what makes it true.

Some people equate truth to morals as in, good people tell the truth, and bad people lie. That idea is too simple to be accurate. What we should do is find our relationship with our truths and see how we feel when we say them out loud. There's that quote, "Speak your truth, even if your voice shakes." I'm more interested in why our voice would shake in the first place, or maybe that's what those earlier paragraphs were about.

The only person that has to live with yourself for your whole life is you, so speak the truths that allow you to feel good about your existence. The truth may not set you free, but it will teach you a whole lot about the cages you're in.

"THE TRUTH MAY NOT SET YOU FREE, BUT IT WILL TEACH YOU A WHOLE LOT ABOUT THE CAGES YOU'RE IN."

89 HUMBLE THE DANCER

Sometimes, the only reason the past seems so heavy is because we refuse to let it go.

Is letting go an easy thing? Of course not, and the things worth doing in life are rarely easy. It's better to understand that the past will keep creeping up on us, and jump on our backs. The choice we have to make is whether we're going to let it hold on and enjoy the ride.

I was at a wedding this past weekend with my family and friends, and while on the dance floor I caught my mind wandering. I was either reliving my past, or thinking about the future, meanwhile I wasn't taking the time to enjoy the moment I was in. I told myself, "You're at a party with people you enjoy, soak in this moment while it's here." And it intensified my wonderful dance moves.

Though many of you aren't amazing dancers like me, the point remains that we have to actively bring ourselves back to where we are. Once we do it, it doesn't mean we won't drift again, because we will. Being present requires continued effort. People don't exactly enjoy effort, and that's why their past is getting a free piggy-back ride.

The past isn't let go once, and then gone forever. It'll continue to reattach, so we have to continue to focus on our present to loosen its grip. It's a struggle, but the struggle is what makes us stronger.

"BEING PRESENT REQUIRES CONTINUED EFFORT. PEOPLE DON'T EXACTLY ENJOY EFFORT, AND THAT'S WHY THEIR PAST IS GETTING A FREE PIGGY-BACK RIDE."

90 CHANGE YOUR SCRIPT

When it comes to our dreams, we're generally either making progress or excuses.

That's one of those truths that people don't enjoy hearing, including myself. I'm working on a music project with the lovely IISuperwomanII, and the process has pushed me to work at her pace, which in turn has shown me that I can work way beyond the limits I thought I had. Moving forward, the old excuses I used to have to 'take my time' no longer apply, as I've realized a new level within my own potential.

This will be an ongoing process for everyone, including myself. We'll continue break through our limits, some of them mental, some physical, some spiritual, sexual, financial, philosophical, intellectual and so on. The fences we're most obstructed by are the ones we build for ourselves. we tend to serve as the prisoners and the prison guards, and the wardens, and everything else in between.

The first step is to simply be aware of the excuses we make. Change your script from, "Can I do this?" to, "HOW can I do this?" It can make all the difference. Try it out with the things you want to do.

Don't feel bad for making excuses, Mother Nature seemed to have wired us to lean towards a life a minimal struggle, progress comes when we disobey that code.

"THE FENCES WE'RE MOST OBSTRUCTED BY ARE THE ONES WE BUILD FOR OURSELVES."

91 WHERE YO REAL FRIENDS AT?

When sh*t hits the fan, you'll learn who really has your back.

We all avoid unpleasant situations, and disappointments, but those moments are when the most is revealed. It's easy to have people around when you're on top of the world, but pay attention to how many of them jump ship the first sign of a leak. This isn't tragic, it's really a blessing. These people are toxic in your life, and you're blessed to have them revealed and out of the picture.

All relationships are based on priorities, and it's too romantic to assume that the people in our lives will take a bullet for us (as we should be great friends, and never put them in the line of fire). It's also romantic to assume that blood means loyalty. Let's all live in the real world. Often relationships form out of convenience, and when that convenience ends, so do those relationships.

How many of us have that friend that disappeared once they got a new girlfriend or boyfriend, only to return to us once that situation fizzled. We need to pay attention to these behaviours, before they bite us in the ass. I've made the mistake of ignoring the actions of those kinds of people, thinking I would be the exception to the rule, I never was. Actions speak louder than words, and let those determine the type of people you surround yourself with

When it comes to friendships and relationships, quality is always better than quantity.

"WHEN IT COMES TO FRIENDSHIPS AND RELATIONSHIPS, QUALITY IS ALWAYS BETTER THAN QUANTITY."

92 EXPLOITATION

I remember being in "love" with a girl, and compromising everything I was to keep her. Years later I realized it wasn't because I really loved her, but simply because I was too scared to lose her. When I first became a teacher, I was signed up for every extra-curricular activity, committee and meeting there was, because I was the new guy, and I was too scared to say no, because I didn't want to lose my job.

I had friends who were taking advantage of me in business, but I didn't ask any questions, sometimes it was because I was too scared to damage the friendship, and other times I was too scared to stare the truth in the face.

When fear is in the room, exploitation won't be too far away.

Fear can be used to control. Some have taught us to be afraid to drink water from the tap so we can purchase their bottled water. Others teach us to be afraid of "the enemy" so we will support their wars. Many convince us to spend two months salary on a shiny diamond, because we're afraid that anything less will tell the woman we love that she wasn't worth it.

When we are afraid, we can be easily manipulated.

The art has been in practice for over a century, and championed by a gentlemen by the name of Edward Bernays (he's the nephew of famous psychologist Sigmund Freud). Bernays is the father of modern marketing, and his ideas were simple; People are emotional beings, and can be manipulated because of those emotions. The kicker is that not only did he put this idea into practice, but he felt that because humans can be manipulated, they SHOULD be manipulated.

Bernays is the reason why every commercial you watch has an emotional element to it. Why a commercial for beer is about a friendship between a dog and a horse. Or why a commercial for a car sounds more like an advertisement to fly to the moon.

On a large scale, or small scale, our fears and emotions can be used against us. It's not a conspiracy, it's simply an effective strategy. What we have to do is be aware of this, and pay attention to when we are being made to feel certain ways.

Are our friends guilting us into doing things? Are advertisers promising to solve problems we didn't even know we had? Are we doing things we don't want to do simply because we're being bullied?

These questions are important to regain the steering wheel of our life, so ask them frequently.

"WHEN WE ARE AFRAID, WE CAN BE EASILY MANIPULATED."

93 TURN THE PAGE

We are writing our own stories as we live them, and every moment is a change to twist the plot, for better or for worse.

Revisiting old chapters in our lives can be both bitter and sweet. We can fill ourselves up with pleasant memories or just drown in regret and desires to take it all back. Either way, that's life.

The past is full of valuable lessons, many of which don't reveal themselves until we wise up a bit (and that takes some time). Those lessons can be expensive. They can take a toll on us, and we can wish away our present by staying lost in a past we wish never happened to begin with.

Every day is a new day, and a new page in the book of our lives, and instead of flipping back in the story, let's worry about the page we're writing on now, and what direction we want to take this. You are the author of your own life.

The best way to improve on the events of the past is to live life differently in the present. Then bring all the wisdom we gained from those events with us, to guide our decisions in the future.

Turn the page.

"YOU ARE THE AUTHOR OF YOUR OWN LIFE."

94 CURVEBALLS

I just got back from Peru, and for most of the trip I suffered from altitude sickness (Toronto at it's highest is 210m above sea level, Cusco is 3300m). That made things difficult because I didn't have the energy to do much, but I didn't have time to delay any of the treks. I told myself to sign up for some suffering and soldier through, and I totally did. Was that a wise decision? I don't know. I've been home for twenty-four hours and the rooms spins when I get up too quickly, but hopefully I'll recover soon.

We don't know our own limits until we test them. Some consider that irresponsible. I learned from my Peru experiences that had I spent more time taking care of myself before hand, I wouldn't have dealt with much of the challenges I did, and if anything, could have pushed harder.

It's not always about what we do at the moment of the challenge that matters, those moments are few and far between. It's more so how we live daily, which shows how prepared we are in those tough times. The curveball life throws won't matter if we've been practicing our swing.

This trip taught me that my mind is more powerful than my body, and it's time to eat better, and stop blaming my travels for my lack of regular exercise, so my body can catch up. It also reminded me that very little is accomplished or achieved straying away from challenges.

All of you reading this are in different circumstances, with different strengths, weaknesses, and areas that need improvement. You don't have to wait until New Years Eve to promise yourself some improvement. Let's all make an effort not to avoid the things that challenge us, and embrace them as growing opportunities.
And as I write this, it's time for me to lie down.

"THE CURVEBALL LIFE THROWS WON'T MATTER IF WE'VE BEEN PRACTICING OUR SWING."

95 RUN TO THE PAST

Maybe it's an old song, a sweater, or a place you visit that stirs up memories of your past. Maybe the memory is painful, of a person who is no longer in our life, or of a decision we really wished we hadn't made. Maybe that pain that comes from reliving those memories is so intense that it ruins the rest of the day, making you want to lie down, or eat unhealthy foods, or continue to spiral into the times that no longer exist.

We can throw away the sweater, maybe find a new route to avoid seeing certain monuments, and we can even delete the songs that rehash the memories out of our lives, but we can't get rid of the memory.

Since we can't run from it, let's run to it and confront it. But instead of just sitting in our memories, let's examine them. Let's ask ourselves, "Why does this bother me so much? What can I learn from this? What have I already learned from this?" We may end up finding things of benefit that can help to balance out the regret. We can find, or create, silver linings because all of our growth comes from our struggles.

No one regrets the pain of the gym if the results are beginning to show. Maybe if we focus on the lessons we learned during those times, and figure out the best way to apply those to our future, we may find ourselves better off. Maybe if we actively focus and remind ourselves to change the channel, we can lead a more positive existence.

Use what is useful from the past, and let go of the rest. If the memories creep up (and they will), burn some calories to push back. Re-shift the focus.

"WE CAN FIND, OR CREATE, SILVER LININGS BECAUSE ALL OF OUR GROWTH COMES FROM OUR STRUGGLES."

96 HUMBLE VS. LOVE

If it doesn't last, can we even call it love? There's such a romanticized view of love, that's all-powerful and unconditional, but how often are we actually experiencing that in real life?

How often do we feel pressured to make our loved ones happy? If they already loved us, shouldn't they be happy with who we are? How often are we imposing expectations of our loved ones that we hope they live up to?

I know this isn't the case for everybody in your life, but that's exactly my point. There are people in our lives who love us for who we are, and though they want the best for us, they also allow us to figure those things out with their support. That's a far cry of the relationships we keep that require so much maintenance and obligation just to keep them running.

People can only be disappointed in us if they had expectations for our lives. It's not our job to live up to their expectations, that's what their life is for. Often, we mix these ideas up and feel guilty when we let our loved ones down; but when did love allow guilt into the equation? How could someone that loves you make you feel guilty about anything?

I'm not here to criticize love, or peoples romantic views on it, but the people in your life may hold the love you have for them hostage. Bottom line, you get to have your own definition of love, and once you define it, let it set the bar for the type of people you allow into your life. This is absolutely easier said than done, but this is your life and you deserve better than anything less.

"BOTTOM LINE, YOU GET TO HAVE YOUR OWN DEFINITION OF LOVE, AND ONCE YOU DEFINE IT, LET IT SET THE BAR FOR THE TYPE OF PEOPLE YOU ALLOW INTO YOUR LIFE."

97 TWENTY-SEVEN AND NOT DEAD

I think we all enjoy feeling special, whether it's a family member acknowledging our accomplishments, or gaining a few more followers on social media. One way for an artist, especially an artist who isn't making much money, to feel special, is by dying at the ripe age of twenty-seven.

It's called the 27 Club, and it's full of celebrities and creatives who, for one reason or other, died at twenty-seven.

Some of the notables in the club include;

Brian Jones
Jimi Hendrix
Janis Joplin
Jim Morrison
Jean-Michel Basquiat
Kurt Cobain
Amy Winehouse

So when I hit twenty-seven and didn't die, as you can imagine, I didn't feel very special, I was lost. I'm being serious.

We all have benchmarks of success, and most of those milestones and finish lines are based off of what other people we see have accomplished. To be a great, and often misunderstood artist (which clearly I am :P), I needed to die in a blaze of glory far too soon, and in my prime.

What I later (and thankfully) realized, was that I wasn't close to my prime, nor does looking at the successes of others every often serve as a good goal for yourself. We are all on our own journeys, and what works for one person may not be the best for another.

We can't look at what makes others special and want that for ourselves, because then it's no longer special, to be special by definition is to be unlike others. We all have something within us to be special, and we can't fake it simply because we want what others have. Society has already perverted the idea of being special, but that's another chapter in itself.

Let's instead explore why we need to feel special in the first place, what are we trying to make up for, and will taking this route ever make us happy. Now that my twenty-seventh birthday has come and gone, I no longer want to die in a blaze of glory, but I won't lie, I am curious how that would affect my art if I went out like Biggie or Pac, but at that point I guess it really doesn't matter.

"WE CAN'T LOOK AT WHAT MAKES OTHERS SPECIAL AND WANT THAT FOR OURSELVES, BECAUSE THEN IT'S NO LONGER SPECIAL, TO BE SPECIAL BY DEFINITION IS TO BE UNLIKE OTHERS."

98 MARKERS AND LABELS

There's only one you.

The way we identify ourselves is interesting, because there are so many ways we can do it. How we identify and then project our persons into the world does a lot to determine how we feel about ourselves.

Some of us identify ourselves based on the markers that were given to us (nationality, ethnicity, and so on) and a host of other labels that our respective societies created. These, as we know, fit us neatly into an organized system for categorization. Some folks spend their entire lives living up to these definitions and labels, because they don't know another way to exist.

I think it's important to note that our value doesn't have to relate to our own identities. Our value comes in our existence, and the simple miracle of being here. A lot of people may want us to fit in, but everyone else is trying to do the same thing. No one fits in exactly, ever, and the problem isn't us, it's the dumb idea that we need to in the first place.

Look inside, and figure out who you are, and who you want to be. Understand those definitions from within will change with time. If you're eighteen and think you got it all figured out, trust me you don't. If you're thirty-five, and think you've got it all figured out, then in some ways you're worse off than the eighteen-year-old.

Let life happen, and flow with it, and while on that journey, discover you're authentic self, that's the self that's going to feel best in your skin, and share that with the world. Who gives a f*ck if people get it or not, they're too busy trying to impress everyone else too.

"NO ONE FITS IN EXACTLY, EVER, AND THE PROBLEM ISN'T US, IT'S THE DUMB IDEA THAT WE NEED TO IN THE FIRST PLACE."

99 GRAVITY

Success isn't about waiting around for results, it's about having a relationship with the process for the results to come. This fast food culture we have doesn't help much to strengthen our patience. We want things to happen now, and get frustrated when they don't materialize quickly enough.

Most of the celebrities and superstars we know of and celebrate were on the grind for years well before they made it into the public eye, we always forget about that. Athletes are training all year, even if the official season only lasts a few months. Even relationships aren't created instantaneously. They take time, and are built piece by piece.

If you have high expectations coupled with low patience, be prepared to be continually disappointed. Don't be afraid of the time that it takes to accomplish things. The time, however, spent, will pass regardless. Nature doesn't move at our pace, we're subject to its movements and the laws that govern it. The more we understand and respect the nature of time, the better equipped we are to benefit from what it can offer..

The moment we understand and respect how gravity works is when we begin to fly.

"THE MOMENT WE UNDERSTAND AND RESPECT HOW GRAVITY WORKS IS WHEN WE BEGIN TO FLY."

100 OSAMA

After 9/11, the most popular beard-and-turban on the planet was Osama Bin Laden, and he provided the context for anyone who looked that way. What's interesting is that to this day, it isn't always meant to be an insult.

The first time I encountered my first "Osama" was in 2001, outside a restaurant, talking on my cell phone. A girl, who was clearly drunk, was being guided by her guy-friend to their car. She noticed me, stopped, and began walking towards me, politely asking, "Excuse me? Are you Osama Bin Laden?"

Her friend was mortified and quickly grabbed her, and lead her to the car, giving me a face that read, "I'm really sorry dude, please just let it go." I think at that point I had so many friends who had shared their similar experiences, that I was waiting for it to happen, as if the vacation from racism I had experienced in my childhood was over, and it was back to being an outsider.

The next time was when a Pakistani guy was trying to bait me into a fight. The fight was over a girl his friend used to see, who was a friend. Alcohol was involved, and I guess he figured it would push my buttons, but all it really did was confuse me. It was a poor attempt to bring me into a problem I had nothing to do with. I didn't expect someone who was Muslim to be calling me Osama, but again, when alcohol and a broken heart are involved, anything can happen. All these experiences were perplexing at best… And then I went to Cuba.

In 2003, the country was littered with anti-American propaganda. There was a billboard on the road showing Uncle Sam groveling to Fidel Castro so – you get the context of how they were feeling. When I was out and about on any given day, I received cheers and would see people screaming at me, "OSAMA!" with giant smiles on their faces. An enemy of their enemy was definitely their friend.

This wasn't the last time either.

In Thailand, many people would scream "Osama" my way with a bit of a smile. As I walked the streets of Lima, Peru, I could hear the adults saying it underneath their breath. In the Dominican Republic, a street vendor came up to me and continually referred to me as Osama as he gave his sales pitch. I asked him if thinking I was Osama was a good thing or bad thing. He replied that it was good, as he hated America because they destroyed his native country of Haiti. The name holds weight and is associated with a monster, a hero, and a mythical character. It all depends on who you're asking.

With fresh incidences labeled at terrorist attacks recently occurring, most notably in Paris, the meaning of my turban and beard will continue to change depending on the beholder. I don't take any of it to heart; the fact that the spectrum is so wide fascinates me.

Being different has always been a blessing and curse for me. It's exhausting standing out, but it's not very enlightening and educating. Blending in. As appealing as it sounds sometimes, it does me little good in learning about the world around me, and although it can be convenient to be an fly on the wall, being at the centre of it all provides a lot of valuable experience.

Depending on when you read this, Osama may be the new Hitler, or just another name in your history textbook. Hipsters are making beards cool, and I don't notice as many stares as I did ten years ago. In that decade, I also travelled significantly, and my biggest take away is that people see world differently everywhere you go. It doesn't matter if they see me in a positive or negative light, what matters is that there is more than way to look at things.

Everything we encounter in life can be seen from different angles. Some of those angles will make things look great, while others will have us running in the opposite direction. Being aware of the power of our perceptions goes a long way to take control of them and decide what lens we want to see the world through.

I'm glad I don't fit in, and I'm more than happy to internalize a few slurs here or there. The discomfort that comes with that is good for me, I learn from it, grow from it, and connect with others based off it. How do you see the world?

"BEING DIFFERENT HAS ALWAYS BEEN A BLESSING AND CURSE..."

101 DUKH DARU

The catalyst of Sikh Philosophy, Baba Nanak, wrote some epicness...

The Gurmukhi expression is;
"Dukh daru sukh rog bhaia ja sukh tam na hoi."

And the English translation reads;
"Pain is the medicine, and comfort is the disease."

It's really interesting considering this was written for an audience in rural India in the 1500's. It's still relevant over five hundred years later.

Safety and security are things we often aspire to, it's one of the main reasons our parents want us to be doctor-lawyer-engineers. The funny thing is, to be able to accomplish these kinds of goals, we have to work our asses off. Good things come to those who hustle, and our biggest obstacles end up being our own need for comfort.

That need for comfort can be extremely expensive. Comfort is what we're used to, it's not what's best for us, or even what will keep us happy. Some people remain in miserable situations simply because it's familiar, and there's a strange comfort to that.

Life exists outside your comfort zone, you don't need me to tell you this, you've lived it. Every time you chose to venture away from (or were yanked out of) your comfort, you were put in a position. Muscles grow with resistance, same with other aspects of our lives.

Think about what comfort means to you, think about what happiness means to you as well. Think about being content, think about being complacent, is there a difference?

The line is blurry, but there is a difference, and that difference is unique to all of us.

As Baba Nanak showed, this idea isn't anything new or revolutionary, we just need the reminders.

"PAIN IS THE MEDICINE"

"COMFORT IS THE DISEASE"

Thank you for taking the time to check out my work, please share this with somebody that you care about, or somebody that you don't; either way I appreciate you spreading the word. =)

Let's Stay Connected

youtube.com/humblethepoet

twitter.com/humblethepoet

instagram.com/humblethepoet

fb.com/humblethepoet

unlearnbooks@gmail.com

All content copyright its respective owners
All written content is copyright of Kanwer Singh
Cover image by Carolyn Tripp
Jacket design by Kanwer Singh and Carolyn Tripp

Made in the USA
Charleston, SC
04 December 2015